Darling, You Were Wonderful

Darling, You Were Wonderful

Harvey Sabinson

Henry Regnery Company•Chicago

Library of Congress Cataloging in Publication Data

Sabinson, Harvey.
   Darling, you were wonderful.

   Includes index.
   1. Sabinson, Harvey.   2. Press agents—United
States—Biography.   I. Title.
PN1590.P7S2   792'.092'4   76-55659
ISBN 0-8092-7872-3

Published by Henry Regnery Company
180 North Michigan Avenue, Chicago, Illinois 60601
Manufactured in the United States of America
Library of Congress Catalog Card Number: 76-55659
International Standard Book Number: 0-8092-7872-3

Published simultaneously in Canada by
Beaverbooks
953 Dillingham Road
Pickering, Ontario L1W 1Z7
Canada

Contents

Acknowledgments

I owe my gratitude to Hayes B. Jacobs of The New School for his constructive advice and encouragement; to the late Ingram Ash, a true hero of the theatrical wars, whom I miss more than I can say; to my friends at the League of New York Theatres and Producers, the Association of Theatrical Press Agents and Managers, and the William Morris Agency; and particularly to my wife, Sarah, who, although she is a professor of mathematics, is the most astute theatre person I know and has an abundance of the love and patience that a writer needs from the one closest to him. Thanks are also due my ex-partners, Lee Solters and Sheldon Roskin, for putting up with me through all those insane years.

Harvey Sabinson
South Egremont, Massachusetts, 1977

Prologue

Stick with Me, Baby, I'll Make You a Star

I understand that Lillian Hellman was, briefly and early in her life, a theatrical press agent. So were the late Russel Crouse and S. N. Behrman. Neil Simon once worked in the publicity department of a film company. Evidently, they figured that they had better things to do with their time and talent, so they took to writing—mainly plays. But they abandoned an honorable, if sometimes misunderstood, profession.

I guess I exhibited more endurance—or is "stubbornness" the word I'm seeking?—than Miss Hellman or the Messrs. Crouse, Behrman, and Simon. I lasted for twenty-seven years and more than 250 productions before I figured that I had better things to do. I tell you this to certify my credentials as an authority on theatrical press agentry.

A great many people go into the making of a theatrical event. There are the ones you all know about: the actors, the writer, the director, the designers, the producer. And there are others only slightly less central to the event: the backers, the stagehands, the stage managers, the business managers, the box office treasurers, the ushers, the ticket-takers, the telephone operator, the hatcheck girl, the stage doorman, the man who sells orange-flavored water in the back of the theatre because there isn't enough space in the lobby, and don't let me forget the lawyers and accountants and secretaries, and go-fers (they go for coffee and Danish for everyone above them). Which brings me back to press agents.

Chances are it's the press agent who got you to the theatre in the first place. Don't tell me it's the star or the playwright or the subject matter of the play. It's the press agent. He or she (as many are women in this most democratic of endeavors) told you that such-and-such a star was coming in such-and-such a play by such-and-such a playwright about such-and-such a subject. He or she did it by getting stories into the papers, by staging clever stunts, by composing an occasionally terrific, seductive ad, by arranging interviews on television and radio, by having flyers and posters printed, by trying to capture your interest in any way possible.

Webster's New Collegiate Dictionary does a reasonable job of defining these creatures and what they do. A press agent is "an agent employed to establish and maintain good public relations through publicity." Publicity is "an act or device designed to attract public interest; specifically: information with news value issued as a means of gaining public attention or support." Isn't that nice and clear?

I figure that forty million people were attracted to productions that I handled, and there's no way you can prove me wrong. My ex-partner, Lee Solters, figures eighty million, but he always tended to exaggerate.

I'll let you in on a secret. Press agents have one shortcoming. If the show they are representing is dreadful, there is little they can do to prolong its existence. They can give a helpful nudge to a show that's on the fence. And if the play is a whopping success, they can take bows. But an outright turkey is beyond saving.

Isn't it the same in any business? The Ford Motor Company's publicists, assigned to promoting the Edsel, undoubtedly busted their gaskets introducing that car, but it was a flop. White House press staffs, through three administrations, tried to sell us the Vietnam War, but eventually they had to fold it.

Can press agents make stars out of nobodies? You bet they can. To support my contention, I'll tell you the story of several nobodies who, fortunately for them, crossed paths with me, and soared to the top.

The first was Carol Channing. I met Carol in the fall of 1948. She was in the cast of a mostly topical revue called *Lend an Ear*, and I was an apprentice press agent with the show. No one performer in *Lend an Ear* was supposed to be any more important than any other. The production had started in Pittsburgh, played a small theatre in Hollywood, and was now opening at the National Theatre in New York.

In a sketch called "The Gladiola Girl," a satire on the musicals of the 1920s, Carol played a dopey chorus girl stuck way back in the third row. But she proved to be the quintessential flapper, larger than life itself. The big round eyes, the almost-but-not-quite vacant stare, a few wisps of bobbed blonde hair escaping a silly cloche hat, the nearly knocked knees visible below a high-cut skirt, it was all there and the audience loved it.

Two minutes into "The Gladiola Girl" and the first-nighters had eyes for no other performer. Broadway had a new star to adore. And for the next few months the publicity office's phones rang incessantly with requests from the press to do interviews and photo layouts on Miss Channing. And do you know who answered all the phone calls? I did, do you hear! Me!

My boss, Sam Friedman, and I were having a field day.

Carol Channing was making us look good and we were doing her no harm either. Then along came that lousy Herman Levin.

Herman Levin is a producer, a good producer. He was preparing a musical version of Anita Loos's *Gentlemen Prefer Blondes*, with music by Jule Styne. Being no dummy, he thought Carol Channing would make a great Lorelei Lee. So he stole her away from *Lend an Ear* and from Sam and me, built his show around her, and made a lot of money. And after the buildup we'd given her!

Carol, however (unlike some others I've met), is no ingrate. After her salary had increased and she could afford it, she had the good sense to hire me as her personal publicist, and we lived happily ever after—or at least until I quit the publicity business.

In 1953 I was associate to another press agent, Karl Bernstein, and we were assigned to work on a Cole Porter musical titled *Can-Can*, with an original libretto by Abe Burrows. *Can-Can* took place in Paris, so Cy Feuer and Ernie Martin, the producers, figured they'd score a coup when they signed a French musical comedy actress named Lilo (don't ask me her last name; for all I know she had none) to play the starring role.

Mind you, nobody in this country had ever heard of Lilo, and I'm not too sure that she was known by very many Frenchmen. "Don't worry," Feuer and Martin advised Karl and me, "she'll be sensational and become a tremendous star. You won't have any trouble publicizing her."

On opening night Lilo faded into the scenery while the show's lead dancer, a high-kicking redheaded phenomenon named Gwen Verdon came on like gangbusters. Her "Can-Can" number was the greatest thing since La Gouloue, and the audience would not stop applauding after her exit.

I was standing at the back of the house next to Michael Kidd, the show's choreographer, drinking in all the excitement. "I'll be back in a minute," he said to me as he dashed down the side aisle and through the stage door.

The unknown Gwen Verdon was in her dressing room to make a quick change before her next number, but the show could not continue until she had acknowledged this spectacular ovation. Kidd rushed in, grabbed her by the hand, and threw her onstage to take a bow. A towel fetchingly clutched against her elegant torso is all there was between the audience and Miss Verdon's naked body. If the number itself didn't do it, this certainly locked it up. Goodbye, Lilo; hello, Gwen Verdon.

But remember—it was I who was standing next to Michael Kidd, and it was I who answered all those subsequent phone calls requesting interviews.

It takes guts for an actor to make his Broadway debut under his own name, particularly when that name is as untheatrical as Jim Bumgarner.

Jim Bumgarner played a Navy judge in *The Caine Mutiny Court-Martial*, by Herman Wouk, based on a portion of his best-selling novel, *The Caine Mutiny*. Bumgarner was never offstage during the course of the play, but he did not have a single line to speak. He just had to sit there, a look of intense involvement on his face, as he listened to all the testimony that was being offered by more fortunate actors. A neat trick for a tyro.

On opening night nobody paid any attention to Jim Bumgarner. Why should they? After all, he had heavy competition from the show's stars, Henry Fonda and Lloyd Nolan. In fact, Bumgarner was so much in character that he went unnoticed for the entire run of the play, which was about one year.

Well, he didn't go entirely unnoticed. I noticed him. More exactly I noticed his name.

"Can I tell this kid to drop the 'Bum'?" I asked Karl Bernstein one day.

"Mind your own business," he replied.

So I never told Jim Bumgarner how I could make him a

star. But he must have read my mind. Yes, I'm sure he did. After the show closed, he became James Garner, and that made him very rich. And when he reads this, he'll know whom to thank.

In the fall of 1954, Karl sent me to what was then known as Idlewild Airport (now JFK) to greet the all-British cast of *The Boy Friend,* an English musical based, like "The Gladiola Girl," on the musicals of the 1920s. Nobody in the company was familiar to me. Not only weren't we getting British names, we weren't even getting the original London leads. They'd sent over an attractive teenager, with a music hall background, to do the Polly Browne role. Her name was Julie Andrews.

I will not keep you in suspense. Julie Andrews was incredible in *The Boy Friend,* and her opening-night reception ranked with Carol's and Gwen's. Again the phones in our office rang. And soon I was working hard to make Julie Andrews a household name throughout the United States. Writers were begging me for interviews. I was the King of Broadway, when—and you won't believe this—along came that lousy Herman Levin again.

This time he was producing a musical based on Shaw's *Pygmalion,* a ghastly idea, and he figured that Julie Andrews, *my* Julie, would make a terrific Eliza Doolittle in what he was going to call *My Lady Liza.*

Levin stole Julie Andrews from *The Boy Friend,* and from Karl and me who had made her a star, put her name up in lights opposite Rex Harrison's, renamed his show *My Fair Lady,* and cornered the market on all the money in the world. Levin could have danced all night, but I cried. After all, I was the very first American to speak to Julie Andrews.

Only a true theatre buff would remember a play called *Little Moon of Alban.* All right, so you remember. Then tell me the name of the young actor who played Julie Harris's ill-fated Irish revolutionary lover in that bomb—the one who was killed off in the first act. Give up? It was Robert Redford.

Little Moon of Alban opened on Broadway in 1960, three weeks before Christmas. It closed one week before that same Christmas, which is the kind of present actors in flop plays usually receive. With less than three weeks at my disposal, I was powerless to make Mr. Redford an overnight star. But I was impressed by his performance. So was my client, David Merrick.

I cannot honestly remember recommending Redford to Merrick. With Merrick you didn't have to. He knew everything that was going on in the business anyway.

It took almost a year for the producer to come up with a show that could utilize Redford. It was called *Sunday in New York*, a small romantic comedy by Norman Krasna. It was a nervous hit, which in the trade means that it might get a respectable run but is too fragile to survive one or two weeks of rotten business. As it was, this one ran almost six months, and I don't recall that there was a mad rush to Redford's door. At least my phones weren't overburdened with requests for interviews.

Another year passed. Then I was given a third shot to propel Mr. Redford into the stellar regions. He was cast as the male lead by producer Saint-Subber in a play that was going to sneak preview at the Bucks County Playhouse in Pennsylvania.

Remember *Nobody Loves Me*? If you say you do, you must be fibbing. Nobody has ever heard of *Nobody Loves Me*, except those of us who were involved, and a few thousand people who saw it during that brief spring spawning season on the Delaware River. But *Nobody Loves Me* went on to become one of the all-time comedy hits as *Barefoot in the Park*. Now there's a familiar title. Neil Simon wrote it, and Mike Nichols directed it. It was Simon's second produced play and the first to be directed by Nichols for Broadway. I think we played in Bucks County under an assumed name because no one was too sure that Nichols could handle the job.

Like most of Simon's comedies, *Nobody Loves Me,* or *Barefoot in the Park,* was a smash from the start. Not much revision was required before we regrouped the cast, which, in addition to Mr. Redford, included Elizabeth Ashley, Mildred Natwick, and Kurt Kasznar, for a normal pre-Broadway tour in the fall before coming to New York.

Following the Washington opening at the National Theatre, accompanied by my associate, Harry Nigro, I went backstage to visit Redford. Harry had told me that Bob was miffed because Liz Ashley was getting most of the publicity. Now that is already circumstantial evidence of star quality.

We had a pleasant discussion, at the end of which I said, "Don't worry about a thing, Bob. You're going to be a big movie star some day."

A remark like that occasionally works. At least it serves to soothe the savage actor. "Aw, c'mon," he said, a look of disbelief on his face. It was about as much as I wanted to hear anyway, so I took it as my cue and retreated.

As Harry and I were walking down the alley toward E Street, my trusty aide said to me, "He thinks you're full of shit."

"I don't care what he thinks," I shot back. "I just wish I had ten percent of his future earnings."

Redford made it all right. And it is to my everlasting credit that I did absolutely nothing to stand in his way. He left Broadway to do the film version of *Barefoot in the Park,* ending a great stage career, perhaps forever.

Already minus the middle "a" in her first name, Barbra Streisand entered my life in 1962 when David Merrick cast her in the supporting role of a garment center secretary named Miss Marmelstein in the musical, *I Can Get It For You Wholesale.* "Miss Marmelstein" was also the name of a song she sang that tore down the house.

Out of Brooklyn, by way of a few club dates and off-Broadway, Barbra was so commanding a stage presence that she overshadowed the show's star, Elliott Gould. (He later attempted to equalize the relationship by marrying her.)

One night, in the Philadelphia tryout, I was standing backstage when Barbra came down the stairs from her dressing room with her manager, Marty Erlichman. She'd already wowed the Philadelphia critics. "Whattya think?" she asked me. "Should I get a nose job?"

"No," I replied.

Reflect for a while on that response. What if I had said "Yes," and she had had the operation? Wouldn't she be just another pretty girl from Brooklyn?

That sage piece of advice propelled Barbra Streisand into becoming the biggest movie star of them all. And I gave it.

I think I've made my point. A press agent *can* make a star out of a nobody. Carol, Gwen, Jim, Julie, Bob, and Barbra may not give me the credit. On the other hand, none of them has said that I held them back.

Come to think of it, most of our biggest stars first appeared on the Broadway stage before succumbing to more lucrative film offers. In a career as a Broadway press agent, one is bound to run into many such cases. Sometimes they slip by unnoticed at first. I worked on flop shows in which youngsters like Burt Reynolds, George Segal, Valerie Harper, Billy Dee Williams, Cicely Tyson, and Sandy Dennis played minor roles. At the time, I could not have predicted their exciting futures.

By now you must be thinking, what did this bum really do to earn his salary besides answering the phone, taking orders, concealing his tongue in his cheek, and coming up with monosyllabic answers to career-affecting questions? The answers, I hope, will be found in the ensuing chapters of this book.

There was never a day that I left my office with the feeling that my work, at least for that day, was done. I viewed myself as a salesman of theatre, which is better than selling vacuum cleaners and more honest than selling desert property in Arizona. And while I have always tried to convince myself and my clients otherwise, I was aware that I was limited by the quality of the material I had to sell.

All those young stars with their burgeoning talent, charisma, and physical attractiveness certainly made me look good. But conversely, I made them look good by getting them frequent media exposure, which, like it or not, in the American show business scene is an essential ingredient to lasting success.

This book is comprised of true tales of the Broadway theatre during the period from the end of World War II to the end of the Vietnam War, tales in which I was sometimes a central, sometimes a peripheral character.

In certain chapters I have resorted to composite personalities and fictional names—not so much to avoid litigation, it's just that under the stress of impending disaster, which on Broadway is the norm, some of the smartest people say the dopiest things. Why pin the foolishness on any particular individual?

1

Saturday's Child

In mid-June of 1966, my wife and I returned from a vacation in Spain. On the flight back I worked myself into a frenzy thinking about the piles of unanswered mail, unpaid bills, and unreturned phone messages.

The first day back in any office is not one of life's great thrills. So, after distributing the usual gift trinkets acquired in Toledo to favored members of my staff, and describing the delights of Iberia to the few who deigned to listen, I sat down at my desk to study a list of several hundred phone messages taken by my secretary. "How thoughtful! David Merrick seems to have called every day," I noted. "Didn't you remind him I was in Spain?"

"Yes," she replied, "I told him that every day, but he kept calling anyway. He missed you so."

My eye ran further down the list. "What in the world does this mean: 'They want you to teach at Yale. Call Herman Krawitz'?"

"Yes, Mr. Krawitz called. He's just been appointed head of the Department of Theatre Administration at the Yale School of Drama and would like to know if you'd be interested in teaching a course there in theatrical publicity."

I spoke to Herman, who at the time was assistant general manager of the Metropolitan Opera. He outlined with intense enthusiasm the proposed program, flattered me a little, and, in turn, received an expression of my willingness to participate. "You'll have to meet with Bob Brustein, who really detests the business you're in," Herman explained. "But we've convinced him that publicity is a necessary adjunct to the performing arts."

Robert Brustein, the drama critic and former Columbia University professor, had just become Dean of the Yale School of Drama. Among the many innovations he was to bring to the curriculum was a major in theatre administration, leading to the degree of Master of Fine Arts. The *Yale Bulletin* described it thus: "The aim is to acquaint students with all aspects of theatrical art, so that graduates of the School are not only qualified to undertake special duties, but are also provided with a broad training, both theoretical and practical, in allied subjects."

A meeting with Brustein was arranged for me. It took place in the waiting area of Northeast Airlines at Kennedy Airport while he was awaiting the departure of a flight to his summer home on Martha's Vineyard. The meeting lasted no longer than fifteen minutes. We realized almost immediately that we had many things in common, not the least of which was a serious commitment to the theatre. As his flight was being called, he said he would recommend my appointment as Visiting Professor of Theatre Administration.

I was greatly impressed with myself. No theatrical publicist within memory had ever risen so high in the academic world—so fast. Since I had no previous teaching experience, I spent the better part of the summer preparing a syllabus, developing a logical, coherent presentation of the course, which was to be known as Drama 151, *Press*

Relations and Publicity, "a seminar and laboratory in public relations, photography, community relations, and newspaper and magazine advertising." It was one of those "allied subjects" mentioned in the *Bulletin*.

My appointment, however, encountered a mixed reception from the Broadway community. Before the semester began, I received a letter from one of my principal clients. It read:

Dear Harvey:

After very careful consideration I have decided to give you notice on my account, and you will be surprised at the reason. It is that you are working for Robert Brustein, who is a violent enemy of my kind of theatre, which is the theatre that pays a substantial part of your living. You are aiding and abetting the enemy.

Under the circumstances, unless you drop the lectures at Yale, I am afraid I shall have to get another press agent.

Sincerely,

David Merrick

If familiarizing young people with the *modus operandi* of the theatrical publicist was treasonous, then I would willingly become the Benedict Arnold of Broadway. "Shoot if you must this old grey head, but spare the Yale Drama School instead" became my motto.

But Mr. Merrick refused me my martyrdom. He did not fire me, and to his credit, he later became a financial contributor to the School.

Opening-night nerves are a minor affliction compared to the anxiety I experienced as the time for that first Saturday class rolled around. "You're being unnecessarily dramatic," my wife, an experienced college professor, pointed out. "You know your material backwards and forwards. You've been dealing with it for twenty years. Just speak slowly and clearly. Answer questions simply and honestly. You're going to make a great teacher. You have a marvelous line of bull. They're lucky to have you."

I kissed her goodbye, headed out the door, and started to warm up the car for the seventy-five mile run from New York to New Haven. Sarah came running out of the house. "Hey, you forgot your attaché case with all your notes."

Class was to begin at 11:00 A.M. In my desire to avoid being late, I arrived at 9:00. The School of Drama is located on York Street on the fringe of the Yale campus. Its main building, erected in the 1920s, is a Gothic structure that houses a theatre of standard proportions. My class was to be held in a small annex just behind the main building.

In the past, I had often taken solitary walks through the Yale campus after unusually disastrous tryouts at the Shubert Theatre, a few blocks away. I found the permanence of the Gothic and Georgian buildings soothing to my troubled spirit. Contemplating the enormous amounts of wisdom that had been exchanged and absorbed within these walls invariably put the small tragedies at the Shubert into proper perspective.

That day I decided to take another stroll in search of spiritual sustenance. It was not a good idea. The very thought that this institution predated the Republic sapped my self-confidence. I sought refuge in the small, airless office that had been assigned me in the main building of the Drama School and attempted unsuccessfully to concentrate on my lecture notes. At ten minutes before the hour, I headed for the annex. There, milling in front of the door, was a small group of students. "It's locked," one of them said. "Do you have the key?" No, I did not. What a marvelous introduction. I'd been locked out of the classroom in my debut in the upper echelons of academia.

"How many of you people are registered for Drama 151?" I inquired. All twelve of them were. I looked at those fresh, intelligent faces, eager for the knowledge I was about to impart to them, and asked, "Anybody here have any ideas where we can hold this class? I don't know my way around here."

"What about the Dean's office?" one of them suggested. "It's open and he won't be in today."

This seemed a practical and appealing solution; my first day at Yale and already I'm in the Dean's chair. We all headed back to the main building, making awkward small talk. I seated myself behind the cluttered desk and began. The group was attentive and interested in what I had to say. My confidence returned; my delivery became smooth and unfaltering. I even started to enjoy myself as I dealt with publicity functions and goals, and the basic elements of news release writing. Two hours passed quickly, leaving no time for formal questions.

As I gathered my notes and prepared to leave, a young woman asked, "How did you get into the theatre and what made you decide to become a press agent?"

I remembered Sarah's advice about answering questions. My reply was unadorned and unromanticized. "I had just been discharged from the army and needed a job. My brother was a Broadway producer. He persuaded his press agent to make me an apprentice. And that's how I started."

Was it too pat an answer? Certainly my initial employment was a clear-cut case of nepotism, having little to do with past education or burning desire. Imagine a biology teacher being asked a similar question and replying, "My brother was a biologist and he asked an associate to make me a lab technician because I needed the job." I felt I had set myself up as a poor example to these novitiates, who were struggling through three years of graduate school in order to break into the theatre. They did not seem resentful, however, for they invited me to join them for lunch that day.

Driving back from New Haven, I thought back to other Saturday afternoons when, as a small boy, I began to receive from my father an education in theatre. Pop must have been close to fifty when I was born; we were never certain of his age. He wasn't much more than five feet tall, and weighed about ninety pounds in the long underwear he wore most of the year.

Pop was probably no more than ten years old when he was brought to America from his birthplace in Kiev, Russia. "I hardly remember my parents," he would tell me. "I had to quit public school to go to work, and what education I have is my own doing."

He had respect for books but was no great reader. My brother, Lee, whose recollections are more vivid than mine, says that from time to time he would browse through copies of Eugene Sue's *The Wandering Jew* and *The Mysteries of Paris*. But I recall his reading only the *Evening Journal*.

"How can you even touch that rotten Hearst paper?" my sister, Mollie, the family intellectual, would ask him.

"It's got big type," he would reply, peering over his glasses.

It was strange reading material for a man who considered himself an atheist and a socialist. Pop had strong political feelings, but he was far from being politically active. He was too tired for that. His opinions manifested themselves only when he spoke to me in socialist slogans of the time: "Religion is the opiate of the masses" or "Capitalism is the enemy of the class struggle."

Sports were anathema to my father. In his teens he had tried to become a jockey, but, as my brother tells it, he fell off a horse on the way from the paddock to the starting line. No wonder he lectured: "Sports are a waste of time. They destroy the mind. Stay away from Yankee Stadium or you'll wind up a bum."

Pop was a salesman of supplies to dental laboratories, a job he found unfulfilling. But somewhere in his past he had had a short-lived but glorious career in vaudeville. He even had a few tattered old photographs to prove it. His act consisted of pantomimed comic sketches based on Shakespeare. I remember a yellowing photo of the murder scene from *Othello*.

"That's me, Desdemona," he said, pointing to a be-wigged hag with bulging eyes being choked by a frenzied, burnt-corked Othello, played by his partner, a distant relative named Percy Shostak. "If I'd stayed in show business," he said, "I'd have been a star by now—like Eddie Cantor and Jimmy Durante—who came from my neighborhood."

"Why did you quit?" I asked him.

"We'd be booked in Boston, then Minneapolis, then New Orleans, then back to Philadelphia," he replied. "The traveling expenses weren't covered in our salary. They ate up all our money."

At any rate, the experience left him stagestruck for life. Though he enjoyed vaudeville, he was highly critical of most acts—probably because he thought he could do better. But he adored the legitimate theatre—more because of the players than because of the plays—and Pop's idea of the perfect outing with his younger son was to go to a Broadway matinee.

Virtually every Saturday during the 1930s, we would attend some play or musical or variety show. We would get up early and take the Sixth Avenue elevated train from Washington Heights, where we lived, to midtown Manhattan. There we would visit Gray's Drugstore in Times Square. Gray's dispensed more than toothpaste, makeup, and aspirin. Its particular specialty was cut-rate theatre tickets, which it sold in a huge basement room. It was a true product of the Depression. Broadway shows would send over their unsold tickets to Gray's, where one could usually pick up two decent balcony seats for as little as fifty cents apiece. At that price, even the worst flops didn't seem too bad. A large bulletin board listed the titles of the shows, and Pop would try to make his selections from among the more literate fare. But we also saw a good many empty-headed musicals.

Once Pop bought two tickets to a newly opened play called *Tobacco Road*, about raw life in the South. Ultimately, it would become one of the all-time long runs in Broadway history, but in its early stages, it was struggling to survive. When we arrived at the Forrest Theatre (now the Eugene O'Neill) on West Forty-ninth Street, the ticket-

taker refused to let us in. "You see that sign?" he asked my
father. "It says, 'No one under eighteen admitted.' The
play has lots of dirty language."

"He's eighteen," said Pop, pointing to the thirteen-year-
old at his side. "He's short, like me."

The ticket-taker didn't swallow the story, and we returned to Gray's to exchange the tickets. Curtain time was
approaching, but a sympathetic clerk gave us a pair for
Murder at the Vanities. It was one of those old-fashioned
Earl Carroll revues playing at the handsome New Amster-
dam Theatre on Forty-second Street, now a dingy movie house. There, for the first time, I saw half-draped chorus
girls. The puritan ethic that forbade me from seeing one
show in favor of another, even racier, bewildered Pop.
"Capitalistic censorship will destroy us all," he reasoned.
"The fascists are moving in."

Pop and I must have attended twenty-five productions a
season during that period of my life. I remember seeing
such great players as Walter Hampden, Katharine Cornell,
Eva Le Gallienne, Walter Huston, Bert Lahr, Helen
Hayes, Ina Claire, and Gertrude Lawrence. And plays by
George S. Kaufman, Maxwell Anderson, and S. N. Behrman.

It would be an exaggeration, though, to claim that I was
fully consumed by the theatre at that time. I enjoyed being
part of the audience, but I had no burning desire to become a participant in the production process. At school I
never joined the drama club.

During my early days in college, my brother Lee became
a Broadway producer. His first presentation was a play
called *Counterattack,* about the Nazi siege of Stalingrad.
As the boss's kid brother, I enjoyed certain rights, such as
the privilege of hanging around. I would go backstage and
talk to the actors, most of them newcomers still outside the
glare of fame. These included Karl Malden, Richard Base-
hart, John Ireland, and Wendell Corey.

Counterattack flopped, not miserably, but quietly. Sincere intentions, I suppose, had outweighed good judgment. Broadway playgoers just weren't buying serious war plays in 1943. The swiftness of its demise, rendering so many people unemployed, left a marked impression on me. Yet I still found the theatrical milieu fascinating.

That year I was drafted into the army. Accompanying me to my first post, Camp Upton, was my old theatre buddy, Karl Malden, who had been drafted the same day. On the train to eastern Long Island, we compared orders. "I don't see your name here," I remarked.

"Why should you?" he said. "My real name is Mladen Sekulevich. Never bothered to have it legally changed."

"That's worse than Spangler Arlington Brough," I said, proudly displaying my newfound penchant for Hollywood trivia.

"Spangler Arlington Brough? Who the hell is that?"

I had him. "Robert Taylor," I replied smugly.

Malden spent most of the war acting in an all-GI play called *Winged Victory*. His was an occupation in great demand in the army. Since I was a math major, I was made a mortar gunner in an armored division. But, indirectly, that helped get me into show business.

When the war ended I was a second lieutenant stationed in a Bavarian town in West Germany. Once the shooting had stopped, we drifted into a boring routine of close-order drill, lectures on venereal disease, and softball games. One day the battalion commander called a meeting of his officers to discuss the problem. "The goddamn morale of the men is awful," he said. "We've got to do something quickly or we'll have a lot of goddamn trouble on our hands. I want one of you officers to volunteer for the job of special service officer and think up some goddamn activities to keep 'em busier 'n hell. Have 'em do a goddamn show or something. And if there are no volunteers, I'll pick one of you guys myself."

I raised my hand. "I'll do it, Colonel." It was the first time I had volunteered for anything while in military service. Who was better qualified than I, with my 150 Satur-

day matinees, and a brother who was a Broadway producer? By now Lee had produced his third play, *Home of
the Brave*, another war opus, which had just closed. He
had this thing about war plays. His second production,
Trio, was about lesbian love, far too provocative for its
time, far too tame for today.

Within a few weeks, I had ferreted out all the available
talent in our outfit, including a transvestite corporal who
was a superb belly dancer. We wrote, borrowed, cribbed,
and put together a musical revue that opened at the
Burghausen *Schauspielhaus* for three wildly successful
performances. The specifics of this production have long
since been forgotten. What remains in my mind is the
sense of sheer enjoyment of doing it. It was my most important contribution to the war effort, and it started me
thinking about a career in the theatre.

The army released me in 1946. I had a wife, $300 in
mustering-out pay, no profession, and no job. Mortar
gunners were no longer in demand. Big brother seemed
the right person to tap for advice. "What are the job op-
portunities for me in the theatre?" I asked.

"Don't tell me you want to become an actor?" he asked.

"Hell, no. I'm not pretty enough," I replied. "Besides, I
like to eat regularly."

"What about stage managing, and eventually learning
to become a director?"

"Might be boring watching the same show night after
night from the wings."

"Want to try writing a play?"

"I don't know enough except about the war and I'm not
so sure people really want another war play."

That made him wince. "How about publicity? You
could learn a lot, and you don't have to do it forever. It
could be a springboard to a lot of other things."

The last suggestion appealed to me. It seemed like the
express route to security, or as much security as one could
expect in the theatre.

Lee made a call to his press agent, threatening him with loss of life, limb, and job, unless he put me on the payroll as an apprentice publicist.

"His name is Sam Friedman," he told me, "and he says he'll be delighted to have you work with him. Go introduce yourself."

Sam was warm and friendly. He reassured me by saying, "I don't give a shit if you are Lee's brother. Either you work your ass off and learn something, or out you go."

One becomes an accredited press agent in the Broadway theatre by serving an apprenticeship to a full-fledged member of the Association of Theatrical Press Agents and Managers, Local 18032, AFL-CIO, a small union that doesn't exactly welcome applicants with rapturous embraces. All Broadway shows must employ union press agents for the duration of their runs. The problem is that most of them do not run very long.

Sam signed me to an apprentice contract at fifty dollars a week. In order to qualify for membership, I would ultimately have to present proof of at least twenty weeks' employment each year for the next three. The union didn't much care if you were unemployed the other thirty-two weeks. I took the contract to union headquarters and presented myself to two elderly prune-faced gentlemen, Milton Weintraub, the Secretary-Treasurer, and Oliver Saylor, the Business Agent, for the swearing-in ceremony. While my right arm was raised, Weintraub said, "If you have only eighteen weeks of employment in any one apprenticeship year, and fail to get the other two, you lose credit for the entire year. Only one out of ten shows is a hit. We have a fifty percent unemployment figure. Even after you get your union card, you might be unemployed for a couple of years."

Then Saylor chimed in: "We're probably the only union without a forty-hour week," he said. "That's because you're expected to work up to eighty hours with no overtime pay. And you might complete all the requirements only to be turned down for full membership because children of members get first preference and we have a yearly quota of three."

I sensed that they were suggesting I seek a career elsewhere. When they finished, they asked, "Do you have any questions?"

"Yes," I replied, "may I lower my right arm now?"

"No," was the answer. "We must administer the oath now . . . do you solemnly swear . . . "

As I left their office, I turned around and, in my best devil-may-care Humphrey Bogart manner, said, "See you in three years."

I made by debut as an apprentice publicist with *Finian's Rainbow*, my brother's first musical production. During the pre-rehearsal period, Sam proved to be an exceptional teacher. I learned how to write releases and feature stories, and how to create and execute publicizable ideas. He introduced me to all of his press contacts. By observing and then doing, I was able to cope with the details for which a theatre publicist is responsible.

Finian's Rainbow seemed, at first, a tenuous prospect, since it dealt with such divergent themes as racial prejudice in the American South and Irish mysticism. It was a musical with a message and an integrated cast, an example of what, in 1946, was known as "social significance." The show starred the Scottish singer Ella Logan as an Irish immigrant lass; Albert Sharpe, an actor from Dublin's Abbey Theatre, as her father; David Wayne as a leprechaun; and Donald Richards as a union organizer. The character descriptions alone made the project sound less than promising. Certainly no one in the cast was a "box-office" name.

I recall that Lee and Sam went to the airport to greet Sharpe, who was to be our Finian, on his arrival from Ireland. It was his first trip to this country. When a customs man asked him to open his suitcase, it contained nothing more than a change of underwear and a bottle of

Jameson's Irish Whiskey. Sharpe wasn't planning for a long stay in the States.

During rehearsals, I would sneak off from Sam's office to watch director Bretaigne Windust work with the actors. Windust was a quiet, civilized man who had directed the marathon *Life with Father* and was now staging his first musical. I'd also watch Michael Kidd, a dancer with Ballet Theatre, who was choreographing his first Broadway show, fussing with his dance numbers.

It was impossible for me to determine any correlation between the activity that was taking place in two separate rehearsal rooms. Furthermore, the constant repetition that is the rehearsal process seemed boring to me.

How would they ever get this thing on a stage? It appeared so disorganized, a giant jigsaw puzzle with pieces that did not seem to fit together. Or so I thought.

I have since learned that just about every musical goes through a similar schizoid gestation period.

Finian's Rainbow began its pre-Broadway tryout on a drizzly December evening in Philadelphia. We brought Pop down to attend the world premiere. How could you keep him away? Mom didn't accompany us, convinced no doubt that both her sons would never be more than show-business bums. I have a hunch that the theatre seemed outrageously frivolous to her, a vocation lacking meaning or purpose. But she never came out and said it.

Pop sat with me in the third row center of the Erlanger Theatre, an oversized auditorium on Market Street far enough removed from center city to be considered "out of the way." As the conductor, Milton Rosenstock, raised his baton and led his musicians into the first five or six notes of the overture, the old man leaned over and whispered, loud enough for everyone around us to hear, "It's a smash."

Pop called it right. With an exceptional score by E. Y. Harburg and Burton Lane and a witty libretto by Harburg and Fred Saidy, it was an apparent winner.

We had opened the tryout without the security of having a New York theatre booked in advance. Now just about every theatre owner wanted the show.

The management of the 46th Street Theatre wanted it so badly that they were ready to dispossess their current tenant, a revival of *The Red Mill.* In every booking contract there is a "stop" clause, which permits a theatre owner to give notice to a tenant production that does not achieve a certain box office gross figure over a period of one or two weeks.

The Red Mill was hovering slightly above the stop clause. But the box office of the 46th Street somehow contrived to stem the sale of tickets so that within a matter of days it fell below the critical figure. Out it went, and in we came from Philadelphia.

I recall nothing of the opening night, January 10, 1947. I know I was there, but the details have been erased from my mind apparently by the tension of my first Broadway premiere.

It is a matter of record that *Finian's Rainbow* was one of the great musical hits of the 1940s. The opening performance must have been incredible. But you cannot prove it by me.

I clearly remember, however, the following morning. It was snowing, snowing hard. As Lee and I turned the corner from Broadway into 46th Street, we could see an enormous line of ticket buyers, drawn there by the enthusiastic notices and bravely subjecting themselves to the battering of a blizzard.

"Shouldn't we open the house and let them wait inside?" I asked him.

"Screw them," he replied. "They didn't come to my first three productions. Let them freeze their asses off now."

I was too happy to make an issue and let it pass. I sensed the pain that goes into the making of a Broadway success, but it hadn't touched me yet. Failure concerned me, but on that day it did not occur to me that it would ever happen in my lifetime. The show was a blockbuster. And what better place to work than Broadway?

2

Don't Call Me, I'll Call You—Maybe

"Telegram for Lieutenant Sabinson," said the Western Union messenger as he handed me the yellow envelope and a receipt. He had a crap-eating grin on his face because he knew, as well as I, what was in that telegram. Nobody had called me "Lieutenant Sabinson" to my face in four years.

It was October, 1950. They referred to it as a police action, but the war in Korea was the real thing. It had been raging back and forth across that unfortunate land since June when the North Korean Army crossed the 38th parallel. The United States was frantically mobilizing its forces and calling up its reserves. In a reverie of self-delusion, I figured they had forgotten their most reluctant reserve—me.

I had just begun to win my personal war. After three years of struggling as Sam Friedman's reliable apprentice, I had finally become a fully accredited member of the Asso-

15

ciation of Theatrical Press Agents and Managers. I also had a good job with Karl Bernstein.

Karl and I were about to leave for Philadelphia, where we were opening a new musical called *Guys and Dolls*. "Can't you just smell a smash hit?" he had remarked. "How many hits are you lucky enough to get in a career?" Life was beautiful. At least it was until that telegram arrived.

Once before, after receiving a telegram—from President Roosevelt, no less—I had spent three miserable years with the army, in World War II. I had fought through the Rhone Valley, the Vosges Mountains, through Alsace and Lorraine, the Siegfried Line, the Battle of the Bulge, and Southern Germany, without committing a single act of bravery. V-E Day did not find me up to my crotch in the Elbe River, joyfully embracing some Russian infantryman. I was huddled in a drafty boxcar on my way from Germany to France. Forty-and-eights they called those cars, because they could hold forty men or eight horses. We were fifty men, smelling like eighty horses.

Stalled in a railroad station in Metz, we could hear a voice shouting off in the distance, *"La guerre est finie, la guerre est finie."* It grew louder as word passed from car to car. It was true. The war was over. We started jumping up and down, laughing and crying, kissing, and slapping each other on the backs. That was the last war they'd ever get me in.

Almost a year passed before I was sent to the States, eligible for discharge. The waiting had become unbearable. When I reached Fort Dix for final processing, I was a caged tiger straining to break loose. All I wanted was to become a civilian again, to begin a new life with my new wife. Having conquered the Nazis, I would now conquer show business.

The officer handling the discharge procedure advised us to join the reserves. "If you don't, you'll be surrendering your commission. If there's another war in the future, you'll have to start from the bottom all over again. It's also your patriotic duty to join the reserves. You won't have to put in much time. Just sign up and you'll be out of here in an hour. If you don't, you'll have to watch two days of training films.''

This last argument convinced me. I would have signed anything. And by God, the man was telling the truth: an hour later, I was on a bus, on my way home.

For the next few years I received many letters from the United States Army Reserve, ordering me to attend various meetings. To hell with them. They couldn't touch me now. I was a big-shot theatrical press agent. What did that have to do with the military? I was working long hours. Who had time for such nonsense? All the letters went into the trash. I didn't even bother to have my spec number changed from Reconnaissance Officer to Information Specialist, a secure, noncombatant assignment. I put the army out of my mind and out of my life. Or so I thought.

I finished packing for the Philadelphia trip. It was a Friday evening, and *Guys and Dolls* was to give a preview the following night at the same Erlanger Theatre in which *Finian's Rainbow* had had its premiere.

Under George S. Kaufman's direction, rehearsals had gone very well. The Frank Loesser music and lyrics and the Abe Burrows-Jo Swerling libretto were inspired. Only one question remained to be answered. Would the public and the critics accept a musical based on Damon Runyon's Broadway netherworld, peopled by such characters as Nicely-Nicely Johnson, Nathan Detroit, Sky Masterson, Miss Adelaide, Harry the Horse, and Big Julie?

My hand shook as I opened the wire and read, "You are hereby ordered to report to Fort Jay, Governor's Island, 0600 hours 6 Oct 1950, for final physical prior to EAD . . . "

EAD? What the hell was that? After four years of civilian life, I had lost the knack of deciphering military abbreviations. EAD, EAD, EAD. Then it hit me, like a Sherman tank. Extended Active Duty. I would be in Korea before *Guys and Dolls* ended its Philadelphia engagement. I'd be killed on some desolate hillside before the show opened on Broadway.

I called Karl. "You'll have to go on to Philadelphia without me. Rotten luck, but I've been recalled by the army. My wife will tell you where I am. If I get out of this alive, please hold a job open for me."

That night Sarah and I cried ourselves to sleep. Our firstborn was scarcely a year old and a new one was due in a matter of weeks. What monumentally bad timing! Couldn't they at least wait? "Ask them," she said. "I'm sure they'll postpone it. Tell them about your hay fever. Tell them your hearing is impaired. Tell them you're a happy homosexual. Tell them anything."

We could not have slept much. Before the alarm clock rang at 4:00 A.M., I had yielded totally to despair. A great career in the theatre had been cut short. If I was lucky enough to survive Korea, it would be too late to pick up the pieces. I might as well stay in service and put in my twenty years. Maybe they'd revive Irving Berlin's *This Is the Army* and put me in charge.

Every part of me trembled as I dressed. I was too upset to eat breakfast. We kissed goodbye and I promised to call as soon as I knew anything.

The deserted streets of the city were damp from an all-night rain as I headed for the last subway ride that would take me to lower Manhattan. There, at 5:15, the sky still black with night, I boarded the Governor's Island ferry along with several other frightened retreads. The guards at the Fort Jay slip directed us to a cold, red brick building where we were to have our physicals.

Nothing much had changed in four years. Nothing much had changed, probably, since the Civil War. The same impersonal attitudes. The same sharply barked, dreary orders. The same sense of humiliation at being told to strip down to nothing but socks.

We walked from station to station for assorted probes and pokes, carrying large yellow cards, which each doctor or medic took from us as he checked to make certain we were breathing. It could not be called a thorough physical. Nothing would disqualify me from being thrown to the North Koreans.

"I have a history of hay fever, doctor."

"Yes? Well . . . just move on, mister."

They didn't care. They needed bodies. Uncle Sam wanted me and he was going to get me.

One elderly physician showed some interest after look-- ing at my electrocardiogram. "Sit down, please." I placed my bare rear on a cold stool.

"Do you use drugs or barbiturates?"

"Never."

"Do you smoke more than a pack of cigarettes a day?"

"Seldom."

"Do you drink alcoholic beverages in great quantity?"

"No."

"How many times a day do you have sexual inter- course?"

"Change that question to how many times a week."

"You seem to be in excellent health, except that your cardiogram is erratic. We'll have to take it again."

Once more they smeared my body with their greasy oint- ment, affixed those little suction cups attached to thin wires, pushed a button, and the moving pen began to write.

The second test brought an even stronger reaction from the doctor. "Hmmmmmmm," he said thoughtfully, using a phrase that must be taught to all freshman medical stu- dents. "This is worse than the first. I'm afraid you are in- eligible for active duty. We'll have to give you a medical discharge. Too bad."

Too bad? Too bad for whom? "What is it, doc? Give it to me straight. After what I've been through, I can take it."

"Son, you're suffering from tachycardia. You can get dressed now and return home. If you fill out this form, we'll mail you your carfare."

There have been few moments in my life when I suffered from such mixed emotions. I could not bring myself to ask any further about this dread disease, this tachycardia. Either way I was a dead duck: killed by a communist bullet or cut down in the prime of youth by a heart seizure. Anything with the phrase "cardia" in it had to be fatal.

I quickly dressed and started to run to the ferry, bringing myself up short when I realized that such strenuous effort would only result in my death right there on government property. When I reached the Battery, I headed for a phone booth and called my family physician, who also happens to be my brother-in-law, Hy.

"The army has just released me."

"Congratulations. Is that why you're calling me during office hours?"

"No. They're giving me a medical discharge because I'm suffering from a bad case of tachycardia. How long do I have to live?"

"If you're not hit by a car or by lightning, and if you don't decide to commit suicide, a man of your age and condition can reasonably expect to live until his early seventies."

"But you don't understand," I yelled. "I have tachycardia."

"Schmuck, all it is is a rapid pulse. You were probably so tense, terrified, and upset at being called up by the army, that it showed up on your cardiogram. It's nothing. Go home. Enjoy yourself."

I called Sarah and told her we'd go out that night and have a fabulous, expensive dinner to celebrate my newfound and most welcome psychosomatic ailment, tachycardia. I was too tired, too emotional to go to Philadelphia to see the show.

On Sunday morning the phone rang. It was a friend who had been there the night before and had seen the first performance of *Guys and Dolls*. He sounded much too jovial to be the bearer of good news. In the theatre, one man's pleasure is another man's trouble.

"Where were you last night?" he asked. "I looked for you in the lobby."

"Never mind," I said. "It's a long story. Tell me. How was the show?"

"I hate to tell you," he said, his voice unable to conceal his delight at being able to deliver a verbal karate chop to my one good ear. "It's a bomb. They should think twice before bringing it in. Imagine, songs about horse races. Songs about floating crap games. And a Salvation Army girl for a heroine? They don't make musicals like they used to."

"Well, thanks for calling," I said. "I'm going down on Monday. Maybe they can fix it."

"Impossible. You'll see for yourself."

He half-heartedly wished me good luck and I slammed down the receiver, more dejected than ever. On Monday, with much the same feelings I'd had when I went to Governor's Island, I boarded the train to Philadelphia.

I saw *Guys and Dolls* that night. It was a marvelous, wonderful, brilliant, sensational, fabulous musical comedy. It moved the critics to new heights of enthusiasm, and four weeks later, when it opened on Broadway, it did even better.

I put in three years of honorable service with *Guys and Dolls*. It eventually closed on November 28, 1953, four months after the fighting ended in Korea. My tachycardia never became a problem, but when a telegram arrives nowadays, my hand trembles uncontrollably as I struggle to open it.

3

Sometimes Being a Press Agent Is Like Pulling Teeth

Some of the best publicity about some of the top Broadway hits of the 1950s came out of a dentist's office.

Working for Karl Bernstein sharpened my skills as a press agent. He was a man of experience and deserved repute in his field, although he, like most other publicists, suffered from tension and an alarming lack of security. Karl had coasted through the depression handling some of the biggest George Gershwin and Cole Porter hits. While he ranked with the giants of the publicity world, he was equally known for his frugality. He ran a tight operation, deprived of even the smallest of frills and excesses. He had no secretary, no sophisticated office equipment, not even an air conditioner. Karl knew more about low overhead than a trucker steering his rig under a railroad trestle.

For many years he had made his office with a former client, Vinton Freedley, a major Broadway producer during the twenties and thirties, inactive at the time except for philanthropic activities. The office was prestigiously situated on the fifty-first floor of the RCA building. Karl's room was long and narrow, almost boxcar-like, with a large window at one end. The furnishings were spartan: a few desks, a few typewriters, some chairs, and a basic supply of stationery.

If you wanted to enjoy the benefits of air conditioning in those days, you went to the movies. Only the most lavish business suites were equipped with it. Who needed it anyway, on the fifty-first floor of the RCA building? Just open the window and the cool breezes from Central Park floated in, adding immeasurably to a publicist's creative powers— or his ability to daydream.

Karl was a private man, particularly when he spoke on the phone to his producer-clients. He detested the idea of having his associates listen to his phone conversations. In winter or summer, he would lean precariously out the window, relying on the north wind to whisk away his words of wisdom. He had some kind of blind confidence that the wind would not pick him up bodily and propel him earthward. The man was fearless; he didn't even attach his safety belt when the phone rang.

It was during those days with Karl that I learned that I was totally without the killer instinct. Oh, it crossed my mind all right: just the slightest push and he'd be gone. There wasn't a court in the land that would convict me. After all, he was famous for out-of-the-window phone calls. One push, and it would be all mine, the entire business.

But I couldn't bring myself to do it. Occasionally it would occur to me that perhaps those thousands of people waiting in line to get into the Radio City Music Hall were looking up at a man with a phone in his hand leaning out of a high window. Was he calling in his suicide note?

Part of Karl's intuitive cost-control system was to prohibit his associates from having any discretionary expense accounts. If he wanted you to pick up a set of the evening papers, he usually gave you the exact change. It had its advantage in that you never had to lay out your own money. On the other hand, you never were able to give vent to your imagination when typing an expense account.

One of my predecessors in the job claimed that one hot, windy summer day, Karl, without exact change, started to hand him a dollar bill to buy rubber cement. A passing gust sucked the bill from his hand and out the window. America's leading nonacrophobiac leaned far out and watched his greenback floating gently downward. "Get moving, Al," he yelled. "By the time you reach the street that dollar bill should have landed. Look for it on the Fiftieth Street side, near the Plaza. And don't come back without the rubber cement."

Al rushed out, took an ear-popping ride on the elevator, and returned fifteen minutes later with a jar of rubber cement and some change. To this day he insists that as he emerged from the building and looked up, he could see that dollar bill fluttering toward the pavement. He waited until it landed, walked over and picked it up, not three feet from a traffic patrolman's legs.

One day Mr. Freedley made a rare appearance in our end of the office. He looked concerned as he called Karl outside. A few minutes later the old master returned, shaken, pallid, speechless. He obviously had been given some greatly disturbing news.

Composing himself after a few minutes, he turned to me and said, "Freedley is retiring and giving up the office. We'll have to find a new office and move within thirty days."

That shook me up, too. I had fallen in love with that incredible view of Central Park, the cliffs of Jersey, the power stations of Queens, and the George Washington Bridge off in the distance. Where would we find another view such as this at the reasonable price Karl was paying?

In the following weeks, Karl devoted himself to the search for available space. In the mornings we would discuss the listings in that day's *Times*. His budget was around seventy-five dollars a month, and, of necessity, he had to relocate somewhere in the theatre district. That limited him to older buildings, and perhaps to sublets or shared space.

I spotted a listing for a room in the old Times Tower in Times Square. It was on the fourth floor at the point of that famous triangle. While it had only three walls, it made you feel as if you were the King of Broadway overlooking your domain. The rent was a bit over Karl's budget, and he dismissed it with a brief comment, "Not enough corners." A reasonable reaction from a man who knew how to cut corners.

Then one afternoon Karl returned from the hunt in a state of great excitement. "I think I've found the ideal place. It's at Broadway and Fifty-third Street, over the old Hammerstein Theatre, where Ed Sullivan does his show. I'll take you there tomorrow during lunch." Who else but a veteran like Karl would realize that CBS Studio 2 was originally known as the Hammerstein Theatre?

The following day he took me there. The building was distinctly second-rate, but not yet over the hill. We took an elevator up to the fifth floor and walked down a drab green corridor, stopping in front of a door on which was emblazoned the name: Morton Nusbaum, DDS. The DDS must have the key, I figured.

Karl opened the door and we walked in. A sad-faced man with a swollen jaw was sitting in the small waiting room, which was sparsely furnished in early Salvation Army. Two opaque glass doors faced us; the one on the left was ajar and we could hear the hum of a dentist's drill. Karl motioned me to keep my voice down. In the waiting room's only window I noticed a shingle on which I could make out Dr. Nusbaum's name, backwards. To this day I cannot figure why a dentist would display his shingle in a fifth floor window facing a brick wall across the street. I speculated that perhaps he specialized in ornithological orthodontia.

Karl stuck his head into the doctor's room. "We're here, Dr. Nusbaum." A voice answered him, "I'm busy now. Take a look yourself."

We entered the small, square room on the right. It was empty, dark, and monumentally depressing. Karl sought out the light switch and turned it on, which only made the room less inviting. "Well, what do you think?" he asked. "It's the perfect size and it's only sixty-five dollars a month, including my share of the reception room. The neighborhood is convenient. It's only two blocks from Chock full o'Nuts (Karl was hung up on their nutted cheese sandwiches), and besides, a dentist's office will discourage solicitors."

Karl was never overly fond of those who disagreed with him. Besides, I could perceive that his mind was already made up. What the hell, I wasn't sharing expenses. And there might come a day when I'd get a toothache in the middle of work. After all, what press agent could boast of a resident dentist?

Karl plotted the transfer as if he were Hannibal planning to move his elephants over the Alps. There wasn't much to move—that battered furniture and hundreds of old scrapbooks bearing clippings of past shows that Karl had handled. We stifled the tears as we bid goodbye to our RCA eyrie, and headed west. We were welcomed by the sight of Karl's name in gold leaf on the door of the new office, directly beneath "Morton Nusbaum, DDS."

Instead of New Jersey, Queens, and uptown Manhattan, my view now consisted of stygian nothingness, a gloomy air shaft. Never again would I see the sun setting across the Hudson or the miniature figures of skaters on the Wollman ice rink in Central Park or planes banking to land at LaGuardia. At least never between the hours of 10:00 A.M. and 7:00 P.M., Mondays to Saturdays.

Yet somehow I felt a strange new exhilaration working in these glum surroundings. Although the workday was punctuated by the hum of Dr. Nusbaum's drilling and the intermittent screams of his more sensitive patients, I began to enjoy a period of productivity unlike any I had known before. My news releases were sharp and to the point. My feature stories flowed easily from my mind to the typewriter. Karl and I exchanged good-natured banter for most of the working day, and we giggled and laughed a great deal more than we had in our former quarters.

Karl's clients were impressed by his sense of humor and unmatched originality in moving into a dentist's office. It was a first; it was novel; it had a quaint charm about it.

One day a friend of mine visited me during working hours. "How do you function in a place like this?" he asked. "It's absolutely appalling."

"No, it isn't," I insisted. "I thought so at first, but then I began to develop this marvelous sense of well-being, and my work has never been better."

"That's because you're stoned all day long."

"What do you mean stoned?"

"Listen, I've spent thousands of hours in dental chairs. You're high from whiffing laughing gas from that butcher next door. It's coming in through that space up there," he explained, pointing to a transom high over our heads.

"You must be kidding," I replied, reaching for a window pole. I tugged at the transom, but it was obstinate; frozen in the open position.

I knew my friend was right. I also realized that my days with Karl Bernstein were ending. Another six months of being anesthetized daily and I'd wind up a zombie. I vowed to seek another job.

Since then I have worked in many an office. But there are times when I miss the smell of the good doctor's laughing gas—particularly when my powers of creation and imagination are not serving me well.

4

La Plume de ma Grace

The solid gold pen is gone, lost like the thousands of cheap ball-points that I have mislaid through the years. I regret losing it very much. It was engraved: "To Harvey from Grace." And it was given to me by the most beautiful girl I have ever met.

One of my early mentors repeatedly admonished me, "Don't go near the theatre before Christmas. You may be given a Christmas present by an actor or actress, and it will do you no good. It will only obligate you to concentrate on his or her publicity in order to repay the kindness. A press agent should never put himself in that position."

I took those words to heart, and for my first few years as a theatre publicist, I avoided backstage areas from December 15 until after the start of the new year. I subscribed wholeheartedly to my mentor's philosophy. No one could buy me with some trinket. I was incorruptible. My mind was made up: if presented with a gift by a performer, I would return it immediately to the giver.

There seems to have been little reason for concern. To the best of my recollection, no actor ever gave me a Christmas gift—until that day late in 1949.

I was working on a production of August Strindberg's *The Father*, which starred Raymond Massey as The Captain and the extraordinary Austrian actress, Mady Christians, as the Captain's wife. It was a change of pace for Mr. Massey, who by now had become world famous for his portrayals of Abraham Lincoln. He also directed the play, a grim drama of marital infighting.

At the first rehearsal the stage manager introduced me to the members of the company so that I could briefly interview them for their biographies. With the exception of the ingenue who was to play the captain's daughter, they were a veteran group with wide reputations and innumerable past roles. Researching their backgrounds was a relatively simple matter. But the ingenue was making her Broadway debut. She required and deserved special attention.

She had a soft, blonde loveliness that should be described only by gifted poets. She was exquisite. Everything was in the right place. Everything was perfect—the pale translucent skin, the wide, oval blue eyes. Gazing at her was like viewing a master portrait of some serene Renaissance lady of nobility.

Her stage credits were limited. She was born in Philadelphia and educated at Ravenhill Academy and the Stevens School. She had trained for the theatre at the American Academy of Dramatic Arts and had done some work in summer stock. Only twenty, she was untainted by the rigors of trying to gain a toehold on the New York stage. She was shy, but extremely likable. Or is the word "lovable"?

The play opened in mid-November at the Cort Theatre. On the first night one of the producers said to me, "If it's a hit, I'll read the script tomorrow."

He never had to. The notices were less than enthusiastic, although the critics did single out the lovely ingenue. It was apparent that *The Father* would run a few weeks, perhaps a month or so, and then close. It could not have been a very merry Christmas for most of the cast, faced as they were with the loss of their jobs.

Just before the holiday, a messenger delivered a small parcel to me. It was elegantly wrapped, and it contained a solid gold pen, engraved as I have described it. It was from the lovely young actress.

I was miserable. I realized that this young girl could not be making more than $125 a week. Her expenses for room and board, makeup, and acting lessons had to consume virtually her entire paycheck. It should have been the other way around: I should have given her a present.

It would not be possible to return the pen because of its inscription, and I had no alternative but to visit Grace at the Cort and thank her personally.

I knocked on the dressing room door and her soft voice summoned me in. Not knowing what to say, I poured it out all at once and breathlessly. "I thank you for the lovely pen, Grace, but you should not have done it. I know what you're making in this show and it must have cost you nearly a week's pay. You absolutely should not have done it. How could you afford such an extravagance?"

She smiled at me and said, "Don't worry, I can afford it. So just enjoy it."

I thanked her again, wished her a happy holiday, added some schoolboyish small talk, and left the dressing room in a state of embarrassment.

A few weeks later, relating the story to a friend, I learned that Grace Kelly, the daughter of one of the richest men in America, could well afford that gold pen.

Well, you know the rest of the story—how Grace Kelly became a big movie star, and how she became Princess Grace when she married Prince Rainier, and how she now rules over the smallest country and the largest casino in the world.

A few years ago my wife and I were vacationing on the Riviera, making our headquarters in Juan-les-Pins. We would take short side trips in our rented Peugeot, and one day planned a drive to Monte Carlo. "How would you like a personal tour of the royal palace conducted by none other than her Royal Highness, Princess Grace?" I asked. "I'll call ahead and make a date for us."

"What makes you think she'll remember you?" said my wonderfully sensible wife. "You'll just make a fool of yourself. What are you going to say? 'I was the young press agent to whom you gave a solid gold pen when you did a Broadway show more than twenty years ago'? I doubt if you'll get past the switchboard operator, even if she understands your lousy French."

Perhaps she was right. I never made the call. Oh, I would have all right. But I guess I didn't want to take the chance of being rejected by the most beautiful girl I had ever met.

5

$\mathcal{A}$ Gift of a Name

When I began working in the Broadway theatre shortly after the close of World War II, there was a theatre on West Forty-ninth Street that had just had its name changed from the Forrest to the Coronet. The reasons for this switch are vague. Edwin Forrest, for whom it had been named, was one of America's most famous actors of the nineteenth century. His name deserved to be commemorated if only to recall our theatrical heritage.

I imagine that the conglomerate of wealthy businessmen who purchased the Forrest renamed the house apparently for the sake of change alone. This unwise decision, while it did not alter the course of theatrical history, was surely made out of ignorance, or lack of respect. To these entrepreneurs the theatre is commerce, designed to render a profit. And while I have no great quarrel with this viewpoint, I deplore their lack of reverence for tradition.

In the early seventies two new theatres were completed—the Minskoff and the Uris—named for the construction moguls who built them. I was publicist for a costly failure of a musical that opened the Uris Theatre in October 1972. Mistakenly described as "a musical of the future," it was first titled *Up*. When I inspected the newly erected, odd-shaped marquee on the Fifty-first Street side of the Uris, I suggested a title change. A science fiction mishmash, the show was renamed *Via Galactica* lest all the signs read "Up Uris." Better they should have rechristened the theatre.

In my time, several theatres have undergone name changes. Billy Rose had sufficient ego, when he bought the National on Forty-first Street, to label it after himself. The Fulton was changed to the Helen Hayes; the Mansfield became the Brooks Atkinson (an embarrassment, I'm sure, to the former *Times* critic, since, like Forrest, Richard Mansfield was another nineteenth-century stage luminary worthy of respect; the Hollywood, the Mark Hellinger; the Gaiety, the Lunt-Fontanne. The Adelphi was transposed to the 54th Street Theatre for geographic clarity. On more sober reflection, its owners, the Shuberts, then switched it to the George Abbott, after the indestructible playwright and director, before it fell victim to the wrecker's ball a few years ago.

When I learned that the Shuberts were planning to erect new marquees on the Majestic Theatre on Forty-fourth Street, I wrote a semiserious letter to Lawrence Shubert Lawrence, then head of that theatrical empire, suggesting that it was the perfect opportunity to pay homage to my prolific client, David Merrick, whose persistent producing efforts had garnered considerable revenue for the Shuberts. I even pointed out that in the interests of economy, they could retain the M, E, I, and C from the old Majestic signs, purchase only two Rs and a K, and *voilà*, MERRICK.

A wit in the Shubert office replied that it was a Shubert policy, newly instituted, not to name their theatres after the living, and that if Mr. Merrick's status should change radically in the future, I should so advise them and the matter would be reconsidered.

It seems incredible to me that no Broadway theatres are named for Irving Berlin, Cole Porter, George Gershwin, Tennessee Williams, Richard Rodgers, or Katharine Cornell, to list but a few who deserve to be memorialized in this fashion. The proprietors of motion picture houses are even less sentimental when it comes to immortalizing an almost endless list of film greats. Is there a movie theatre in all of the United States that is named for Clark Gable, Marilyn Monroe, Greta Garbo, or the Marx Brothers?

In 1959 one of my clients, Lester Osterman, bought the aforementioned Coronet Theatre. Osterman, who had moved to Broadway from Wall Street, had not enjoyed great success as a producer. He wisely decided that theatre ownership might be more lucrative than producing, and purchased, all at once, the Coronet, the 46th Street, the Helen Hayes, the Morosco, and the Alvin, whose name, incidentally, is derived from the first syllables of the first names of the two producers—Alex Aarons and Vinton Freedley—who built it in the twenties. Lester called me and said that he wanted to rename the Coronet for Eugene O'Neill. "A splendid idea," I remarked enthusiastically.

"How do I go about it?" he asked.

"By securing permission from his widow, Carlotta Monterey O'Neill, who is executrix of his estate," I replied.

"I don't know her," he said. "Do you?"

"No," I said, "but she has great respect for José Quintero. I could ask him to set up a meeting."

At the time I was also representing Quintero's Circle in the Square, a pioneer Off-Broadway theatre in Greenwich Village for which, three years before, he had mounted a superlative revival of O'Neill's *The Iceman Cometh* with a young actor named Jason Robards, Jr. In apparent violation of her late husband's wishes that it not be presented until twenty-five years after his death, Carlotta O'Neill had permitted a world premiere production of *Long Day's Journey Into Night* at the Royal Dramatic Theatre in Stockholm, Sweden, in February, 1956. When José's production of *The Iceman Cometh* opened at the Circle in May of that year, she was so impressed by it that she summoned him to her apartment and awarded him the rights to stage the American premiere of *Long Day's Journey*. It opened on Broadway in November that same year, and became a smashing success. No one rated higher with Mrs. O'Neill than José Quintero.

I called José, who agreed to intercede with Carlotta. In a few days I received word from him that a meeting had been arranged for Lester and me at Mrs. O'Neill's apartment in the Carlton House on Madison Avenue and Sixty-first Street.

We approached this appointment with a good bit of trepidation. Carlotta Monterey had been an actress of middling fame who was considered one of the most beautiful women in the world. Her romance with, and subsequent stormy marriage to, O'Neill were well documented, but nothing we had heard or read was particularly favorable to her. During the playwright's declining years, she set up a protective wall around him, excluding his friends, theatre associates, and family. She encouraged the impression that O'Neill's mental faculties were failing. But her own stability was questionable. At one point, she had been institutionalized, and there was little doubt that she suffered from periods of paranoia, convinced of a great conspiracy against her. She was a mother figure to O'Neill, who had some desperate need for the kind of woman Carlotta was. Yet the marriage lasted twenty-four years, despite the charges and countercharges that the two hurled at each other. At the end, only Carlotta was with him, sustained by a driving dedication to the man and his work. Her legacy was full control of all O'Neill writings, published and unpublished.

Lester and I had been warned that Carlotta O'Neill was a woman with a short fuse. We agreed that our request must be conveyed with dignity, that we would apply no pressure nor present any persuasive arguments in our behalf. We would merely advise Mrs. O'Neill of our desire to rename the theatre after the most important American playwright of this century. If she refused, we would drop the matter at once.

On a humid night early in August we presented ourselves at the reception desk of the Carlton House, and after
the desk clerk announced us, we were told to proceed up to
the apartment. Carlotta Monterey O'Neill answered our
knock. Although in her early seventies, she was still one of
the most beautiful women in the world. Of medium
height, she was dressed in black. Her jet-black hair was
pulled tightly back. Her dark, searching eyes examined us
thoroughly as she bid us enter a long hallway whose walls
were covered with photographs of O'Neill, alone and with
her, and a number of framed letters. When we reached the
tastefully furnished living room I noticed that it was filled
with oriental antiques, salvaged, no doubt, from the several homes she and O'Neill had shared. With barely a
word of greeting, she turned to us and said tersely, "Gene
would never approve of having a Broadway theatre named
for him. If it were an Off-Broadway theatre—you know he
started at the Provincetown Playhouse—that would be different. Or if a new theatre were to be built. But under these
circumstances, I cannot possibly give you permission."

Lester and I had not said a word about the purpose of
our visit. Apparently our mission had failed before it
started. Would it be polite to leave after so brief an audience? Each of us was confused, and finally Lester said
meekly, "We have no desire to twist your arm, Mrs.
O'Neill. We'll respect your wishes."

As we started to leave, Carlotta, sensing our embarrassment, said, "Please don't rush away. Sit down and have a
drink."

She asked us what we wanted, went to a small bar in a
corner of the room, and poured two glasses of Irish
whisky. As she served us the drinks, she saw me trying to
read one of the framed letters. It was written in a tightly
compressed hand, and was quite difficult to decipher.

"That letter you're looking at," she said. "It's an apology from Gene after he had signed a petition committing
me to a state mental hospital in Massachusetts. They made
him say that I was incapable of taking care of myself. He
didn't know what he was doing. After all, he was in a hos-

pital too, at the time, suffering from that broken leg. After-wards, he was sorry. He wrote this letter." She removed it from the wall and handed it to me.

"Most of these letters," she said, waving her hand around the room, "are letters of apology. Like so many sensitive people he was capable of extreme cruelty. He could be loving at one moment and hateful at the next."

Lester and I glanced at each other and sat awkwardly on a couch facing Mrs. O'Neill. We shared a mutual guilt at having disturbed her privacy, yet it would have been rude to exit hastily. For the next hour or so Carlotta spoke without pause, and we listened in total fascination. "José did a superb job with *Long Day's Journey Into Night*," she said. "I think he's a brilliant young director.

"You know, it's simply not true that Gene wanted pub-lication and production of this play held up for twenty-five years after his death. He'd been persuaded to do so by Eugene, junior, who had some personal reason. After Eu-gene's suicide in 1950, there seemed to be no logic in with-holding its release. Before he died, Gene told me that he no longer wished it to be withheld. Three years ago I gave Yale University permission to publish it, providing the re-venue went for the upkeep of the O'Neill collection at the Yale library and for playwriting scholarships at the Drama School. After so many years of neglect, there seems to be renewed interest in his plays. I'm happy about that."

Then she began to talk about her life with O'Neill in the declining years. "The worst time was Marblehead. I hated that dinky cottage. Gene always wanted to live by the sea. He loved the sea. We didn't have much money, and I paid for it out of a small account I had. He was so ill, and at times it made him violent. We had terrible disagree-ments, and on several occasions he struck me. Then he would suffer great remorse and write these letters asking my forgiveness.

"You know, I've received a great deal of criticism for helping him destroy six unproduced plays after we had moved into that hotel in Boston. He knew he didn't have long to live and would never be able to finish them. They needed revision and he didn't want me or anybody else finishing them. We tore them up, bit by bit. It was as if we were killing our own children.

"It was his early life that destroyed Gene. He wore out his body and soul then. The doctors said he had Parkinson's disease, but it was a hereditary nervous ailment."

During all this, Lester and I barely spoke except to interpolate an occasional "Yes" or "I see." Everything she had been telling us was public knowledge, but it seemed remarkable hearing it from one of the players in this tragic drama. Our shirts and jackets were drenched with perspiration. "Mrs. O'Neill," I said, "we've taken too much of your time."

"Oh, no," she said, "I've enjoyed your visit. Would you excuse me for a minute?" She disappeared into the kitchen and emerged a few moments later bearing an assortment of pots, pans, and salad strainers. "Please give these to your wives," she said, handing these bewildering gifts to us. "I assume you're both married."

We nodded that we were, thanked her, and carefully balancing the kitchen utensils, headed toward the door. As I twisted the handle, Mrs. O'Neill said, "It's perfectly all right with me if you want to call your theatre the Eugene O'Neill. Nobody has asked me this before. Go ahead and do it."

Her sudden decision surprised and elated us. Talking rapidly, Lester explained that in lieu of the usual block electric letters, he would like the marquees to bear a replica of O'Neill's signature. Carlotta was pleased, and offered to send him a copy.

On the day in late September of 1959 that the Eugene O'Neill Theatre was dedicated, I received a small, flat package. It contained a soft-covered pamphlet published by the Yale University Press, entitled *The Last Will and Testament of Silverdene Emblem O'Neill* by Eugene O'Neill. The playwright had written it on the death of his and Carlotta's beloved Dalmatian, Blemie, in 1940 at Tao

House, their ranch in California. This short essay contains, I believe, some of O'Neill's finest writing, and perhaps his ultimate philosophy of life. In it Blemie states, "I feel life is taunting me with having overlingered my welcome. It is time I said goodbye, before I become too sick a burden on myself and on those who love me. It will be a sorrow to leave them, but not a sorrow to die. Dogs do not fear death as men do. We accept it as part of life, not as something alien and terrible which destroys life."

The pamphlet was inscribed: "For Harvey Sabinson —Thank you for those things you have done for me!" It was signed "Carlotta Monterey O'Neill."

I do not know what things I did for her. Perhaps just listening quietly to a lonely, aging woman on a warm summer night meant something to her. I hope so. It did to me.

Nowadays, when I pass the Eugene O'Neill Theatre, I sense some feeling of accomplishment. O'Neill's plays are done with great frequency all over the world; they will never be neglected again. I'm especially happy that there is an edifice bearing his name—a place for people who toil at making theatre, and for those who come to see it.

The Eugene O'Neill Theatre is now owned by Neil Simon, America's finest writer of contemporary comedy. I find great poetic justice in the fact that a theatre named for a playwright is owned by a playwright.

6

"Another Opening, Another Show"

(What you are about to read is true. Only some of the names have been changed to protect the crazed.)

The Crux is opening on Broadway tonight at 6:45, which in the theatre means 7:10. It is a new drama about marital infidelity by Jerome Worth, directed by Kevin Martin, produced by Daniel Gannon, and publicized by me. It stars two former Hollywood actors, Natalie Borden and Philip Carlisle, neither of whom has been able to get a job in motion pictures for the past five years. They play an embattled couple whose marriage starts to disintegrate when she becomes assistant editor of a women's-lib magazine.

After four weeks of rehearsals, during which the original director, Calvin Freedman, was replaced by Kevin Martin, the play opens at the Shubert Theatre in New Haven. Freedman and the playwright have had a difference of opinion. The director saw the play as a bedroom comedy;

Worth views it as a modern tragedy. The New Haven critics label it a monumental disaster.

"New Haven reviews aren't important. I couldn't care
less," the producer says to me. "They're all 'hey-you' critics anyway."

"What are 'hey-you' critics, Danny?" I ask.

"Oh, you know. The editor needs somebody to cover the
show at the Shubert and he looks around the city room. A
young reporter is passing by and he yells, 'Hey you, go
cover the opening tonight.' And don't call me Danny. My
name is Daniel."

"Maybe you're right, Daniel. But it's the review in the
Yale Daily News that disturbs me," I say. "That kid is
sharp and he writes well."

"What are you talking about? He's just a college boy. If
a show has a beginning, a middle, and an end, he'll pan it.
Natalie needs a new dress in Act Two. That should help.
We'll have the costume designer get it ready for the Boston
opening."

The Crux grosses $11,500 for nine performances in New
Haven. We tell *Variety* that a blizzard kept business down.

An eight-inch snowfall greets the show's Boston opening the following week. Gannon and I stand in the lobby
of the Colonial Theatre watching the audience arrive.
"Isn't there anybody here tonight who's under eighty?" he
asks. "They won't react. They won't understand it."

I think to myself, "He's right. It has a beginning, a middle, and an end."

Nobody yells "hey you" to the Boston critics. They're experienced and perceptive. They've spent years as guinea
pigs for theatrical experiments. At eleven o'clock, I head
for the newspaper offices to pick up carbon copies of the
reviews.

"I'm sorry, Harvey. I wish I had liked it," says Elliot
Norton of the *Herald-American* as he hands me his copy.
"Got any new shows coming up?"

I read his review in a cab on the way to the *Globe*. His
lead tells it all: "Last night a melodrama called *The Crux*

opened at the Colonial Theatre. It is a clumsy piece that, at this point, reflects no credit on anyone associated with the production."

One other line jumps out at me: "Miss Borden's second act costume makes her look dumpy."

The *Globe* critic, Kevin Kelly, doesn't have the nerve to face me. He has left a carbon of his review with the uniformed guard in the lobby. I return to the cab and read, *"The Crux* marks a new low for this dismal Boston theatre season."

I read no more and return to the Ritz-Carlton Hotel to present Gannon with the good news. He is in the second floor lounge playing host to the stars, the playwright, the director, and assorted hangers-on.

"You got them already?" he asks.

"Right here," I answer, tapping my breast pocket, hoping he'll get the message and not press the point.

"So read them out loud," he demands.

I hesitate. He insists. I read, looking up from time to time to see wounded faces as they are repeatedly jolted by flailing words.

A long period of silence follows, then Gannon speaks up, "Cheer up. That Norton, he only likes musicals. We have to get to work now. The second act stinks, Jerry. Rewrite it so that Natalie can play the whole thing in a bikini. She's still got a great body. It'll make the conflict between her and Phil more believable."

Natalie winces. Jerry moans. I interrupt. "Danny, there isn't much to quote in these reviews. I'll just run my ads straight."

"Okay," he says, "but put at the top, in big letters, 'The Most Exciting Drama of the Season.' Nothing can stop us from making up our own quote. Have a drink and don't look so depressed. It's gonna be a hit."

"I'd rather have a chicken sandwich, Danny, I'm hungry," I say.

"You can't. The kitchen's closed. And don't call me Danny."

The two weeks in Boston pass swiftly. The author sits at the typewriter in his Ritz suite day and night, rewriting every line, smoking four packs a day, and developing walking pneumonia. The actors meet with the director every morning and rehearse the new scenes. At night they play the old ones. The bedroom set, originally baby blue, is repainted shocking pink. Boston theatregoers stay home watching television. It snows every day. I bail out and return to New York to prepare for the opening. We tell *Variety* that business is off because of a blizzard. They don't believe us this time.

New York is not feverishly anticipating the arrival of *The Crux*. The box office of the Plymouth begins to sell tickets. Eight people show up. At the end of the first day's sale, the treasurer tells me he has read the *Times* from cover to cover—twice.

"You should have sent somebody out for the *Post*," I suggest.

"I'll remember that tomorrow," he says.

The Crux winds up its Boston engagement. Gannon calls me after the last performance there and says, "It's not the same show you saw. The changes are wonderful. It plays like a hit. Now get to work, tell everybody. We need an audience. Oh, one more thing. We're cancelling the Monday preview. We need a day to paint the set baby blue."

Previews start on Tuesday. I watch the play from beginning to end. Damned if Gannon isn't right. The show has improved. The actors are secure in their parts. Natalie looks good in a bikini. It works because it liberates the character of the wife. I begin to believe that *The Crux* has a chance. I must believe it, because there is no other way I can make myself show up at the opening.

On Wednesday morning I meet a neighbor in the subway. I'm trying to read my *Times*. He says, "Of all the people I know, you have the most interesting job. Imagine going to all those openings and meeting all those famous people. You must know the big stars real well. God, it must be exciting."

"Yeah, exciting," I reply, and return to my *Times*.

The press tickets for the opening have been in the mail for a week. During the day five critics call to say that they never received theirs. I yell at my secretary. She begins to cry and says, "But I mailed them all." I tell the critics to look for me in the lobby and I'll see that they're seated in their proper locations.

Gannon calls and asks if the press has returned any tickets. "The backers are driving me crazy. I need all the extras I can lay my hands on. If you get any back, don't give them to your other newspaper friends. Send them over here. I'm a desperate man."

I turn to my secretary. "If we get any returns, send them over to Gannon." She starts to cry. "I mailed him three pairs four days ago, and I even used the zip code."

Somebody from the Channel Seven newsroom calls. "We lost the color transparencies of *The Crux*. Rush over another set by messenger."

I tell my secretary. She says, "I haven't sent out any yet."

The critic from a small but influential daily calls. "I don't mean to make an issue about this, but why did you put me back in row H? It's not my ego that concerns me, but it is difficult to see and hear from H. Can you improve them?" He is in his mid-thirties, his sight and hearing still at peak efficiency. I promise him I'll try. The honest answer would be to tell him that H is exactly where he belongs in the pecking order.

Another reviewer, from a local radio station, calls. "I need an extra single. I want to bring my son."

"How old is he?" I ask.

"Fourteen," he replies. "Why? Is the play dirty?"

"No," I answer. "I would rate it PG."

I do not tell him that there is absolutely nothing on that stage that would interest a fourteen-year-old boy, outside of Natalie's bikini.

Other similar misfortunes pepper the day. Fatigued by all the excitement, I decide to skip the final preview and go home to watch the Knicks on television. The "F" train is stalled for forty-five minutes in the tunnel under the East

River. I read the *Post* from cover to cover—twice.

I finally make it home at eight o'clock. One drink and I fall asleep on the living-room couch. I wake up to see the last five minutes of the game as the Knicks lose to the Kansas City-Omaha Kings, 115-114, in a game played in Des Moines. My wife tells me, "You work too hard. You need a less glamorous business."

I wake up on opening day exhausted. I do not shave because I will only have to shave again that afternoon. I put on my oldest suit and take my tuxedo from the closet. It has egg-drop soup stains on the lapel from an opening night party in a Chinese restaurant earlier in the season. I put it into a plastic garment bag, along with a dress shirt, black socks, and my patent-leather pumps. My wife reminds me, "Don't forget your studs, stud."

"Very funny," I answer, putting the studs into my jacket pocket. I forget my black butterfly clip-on bow tie.

I leave the house in a driving rainstorm. N. Richard Nash, the playwright, once told me, "It's always good luck when it rains on opening day." It might be—for him. He wrote *The Rainmaker*.

The subway ride to Manhattan is agony. The train is jammed. I am an annoyance to everyone around me with my garment bag, attaché case, and umbrella. I even make a valiant try to read my *Times*, but give it up in favor of reading the *News* over a short man's shoulder. He turns the pages too fast.

The day is endless. More small disasters pile up. "You left an important credit out of the program," phones the stage manager. "Can you get it in for tonight? It's 'Miss Borden's bikini by Beach-Togs, Limited.'"

Gannon calls. "Where the hell were you last night? I had a terrible run-in with Phil after the performance. You should have been there to take his abuse. He hates the blow-up of himself and Natalie in the frame near the box office. Make sure it's changed before the show tonight."

"Which one does he prefer?" I ask, knowing full well the answer.

"The one where he's standing all alone looking out the window."

I call my blow-up man. "Jerry, come over right away. I have to give you a photo for a new blow-up at the Plymouth. It must go up tonight."

"Tonight?" he screams. "I can't do it that quickly. It'll cost you double."

I tell him, "All right, all right. So does my same-day dry-cleaning."

The Channel Seven newsroom calls again. "We can't find the transparencies of *The Crux*. Rush some over by messenger." My secretary begins to cry, "I brought them over there myself last night on my way home from work."

"Whom did you leave them with?" I inquire.

"The receptionist. I caught her just as she was leaving."

I phone Ingram Ash, my advertising man, at the Blaine-Thompson Agency. For the one hundredth time I ask the same questions: "Are you ready for tonight? Are all the TV sets in your office working? Have you arranged for all the radio and TV reviews to be transcribed? Will you have a few quote-ad layouts ready to show, just in case? Did you reserve a table in Sardi's? We'll grab something to eat and then go upstairs to your office at 10:30 to catch Stew Klein on Five. You can expect a mob to follow us. I don't know how many. Lucky for us the opening night party is on the East Side. Are you staying in town tonight? If the notices are any good, we'll have to meet at your place at 10:00 tomorrow morning, God and Clive Barnes willing."

"Yes, Harvey, bubi," he says laconically.

"Have I forgotten anything?" I ask.

"Yes, for Chrissakes, take it easy. It's only a show."

I turn to my associate, Harry. "What time did you tell the photographers to come, 9:20? Don't you think that's cutting it a bit fine? Call the photo desks and tell them 9:15. And don't let me leave here tonight without a copy of the first-night press list. You bring one, too, in case you forget to remind me."

The morning wears on. Hunger pangs set in. Time for a

glamorous theatrical luncheon, a liverwurst sandwich and a Tab, deskside. The phones ring with incessant inquiries: "What time does the curtain go up? What time does the curtain go down? When are the intermissions? Can I do a radio tape with Miss Borden and Mr. Carlisle in their dressing rooms while they're making up? Is it black tie? Where's the Plymouth Theatre? Do you have a bio of Calvin Freedman?"

"Calvin Freedman? He's no longer the director," I tell this last idiot.

"I didn't know that. I never read the papers," mumbles the idiot, a drama editor.

A silken voice woos me telephonically, "Hello, Harvey? This is Alice Trinkle. I'm the drama critic of the Grand Island, Nebraska, *Sun-World* and I'm just in town for a few days. May I come see your opening tonight?"

"Gee, Alice," I say. "I wish you'd written to me before you left Grand Island so I could have made the arrangements. I'm all out of tickets at the moment. If anything comes up, where can I call you? What hotel are you staying at?"

"Well, Harvey, I'm moving around. I'll call you back later this afternoon, luv," she coos, and hangs up.

"Listen to me carefully," I tell my secretary. "If an Alice Trinkle from Grand Island, Nebraska, calls this afternoon, tell her I'm out. I never heard of Alice Trinkle, let alone Grand Island."

The company manager is on the line. "I'm gonna depend on you, Harvey, baby, to tell me when to tell the stage manager to take the curtain up. What time did you tell the critics?"

"Seven-ten," I say, "but wait until I give you the word. We must come down at 9:30 because of the early deadline at the *Times*. If necessary, shorten your intermissions. Let them have one puff, and then get them back in their seats. And don't let them clog up the lobby as they come in. All that gawking drives me nuts. Flicker the lights a lot and start yelling 'Curtain going up' at 6:30."

"Helen Hubbell is on the phone," my secretary says.

"Look, Irving, I gotta run. See you tonight. Pray for a hit," I say, hanging up one phone and picking up another.

"Helen, darling, how are you? Are we going to see you at the opening tonight?"

"How come I wasn't invited to the opening-night party?" she fires back, with just the slightest touch of venom in her voice.

"But, Helen, darling, Danny would feel terrible if you didn't come to the party. I can't for the life of me understand why you didn't receive your invitation. It's at the Joie de Vie at 10:00."

She feels better, but I feel worse. No press was invited to the party. Gannon is giving it for the company and backers only. I call him. "Danny, listen. Helen Hubbell is coming to your party tonight. I invited her . . . No, I didn't tell her that it's a private affair . . . Do you want to be on her shit list for life? Do you want me to be dead with her? . . . Danny, try and understand. I did it for your own good . . . No, I won't invite any more newspaper people, I promise, Danny . . . Just Helen . . . Goodbye, Danny-el, see you tonight. Pray for a hit."

I instruct my secretary, "Send wires to Natalie Borden and Philip Carlisle at the Plymouth, as follows: 'Wishing you everything you wish for me. Break a leg. Hope it runs forever.' Sign it Harvey Sabinson. Yes, better use my last name. I'm not sure they know who I am."

My wife rings: "What time does the curtain actually go up? I have to eat, dress, walk the dog, and find a place to park. And I don't want to rush."

I tell her, "Seven-ten, and park in the lot near Ninth Avenue. It's two dollars cheaper. Just run up the street after you park. I'll see you later. Pray for a hit."

"What are you doing about dinner?" she asks.

"Dinner. Yes, I'll do something about dinner. Goodbye."

I look at my watch. It's 5:15. I order my secretary to go

down and get me something to eat. "What would you like?" she asks.

"A broiled lobster," I reply, "but I don't have time. Get me a strawberry yogurt. And don't forget a plastic spoon."

I reach into a lower desk drawer and pull out a small shaving mirror and an electric shaver. I shave while continuing to take calls. When the phone is on my right ear, I shave the left side, and vice versa. One sideburn comes out half an inch shorter than the other.

I go to the john, take a whore bath, douse myself in Aramis, and begin to dress. The tuxedo falls out of the garment bag and has to be brushed for ten minutes. The studs defy my clumsy, nervous fingers, and I seek the help of the prettiest girl in the office. "My, my, aren't you the handsome one," she comments as she pressures the studs into place. The Aramis is obviously driving her wild.

Prince Charming is almost ready for the ball. The pants are a little snug; the tuxedo was purchased about ten pounds ago. The patent-leather shoes are tight enough to keep me from falling asleep during the evening. Everything is perfect, but where the hell is my bow tie? Damn, I forgot to bring it.

Loyal secretary returns with yogurt. "They didn't have strawberry, so I got boysenberry instead."

"It doesn't matter. I really don't like strawberry. Come to think of it, I don't even like yogurt. Except that my wife says it's good for my stomach. Don't take off your coat. Run down again and get me a wide, black butterfly bow tie. At any price."

She returns in a few minutes with some shoelace-like thing that would look funny on a tourist from Oklahoma City. I put it on anyway and, resplendent in my dinner jacket, feast on boysenberry yogurt. "It's only show business," I keep telling myself. "What we did here today will not long be remembered by this world."

It is 6:15, and time to become an active participant in one of the most glittering spectacles known to man, the Broadway premiere. When I leave the building, it is still pouring. I think of playwright Nash's words and mutter under my breath, "Screw you, Dick. I hate your guts."

By the time I reach the Plymouth, the crease in my pants has disappeared and my hair is matted. I wipe the mud stains from my shoes by rubbing them against my trouser legs. No sidewalk gawkers tonight. The lobby, however, is beginning to fill. Irving, the company manager, comes running up to me. "You look charming," he says, "but where the hell have you been? There's a guy over there looking for you."

I peer across the lobby and it's one of the critics who claims he never received his tickets. "As soon as they open the doors, I'll have an usher seat you. I know exactly where you're supposed to be sitting," I say, reaching in my pocket for the press list. But it's not there. Harry has forgotten to remind me. "Just stay where you are," I tell the critic. "I'll be back in ten, maybe fifteen, minutes."

The ticket-taker opens the house and the audience starts to enter. The lobby is jammed now. Gannon arrives and says to me, "What a great-looking audience. They're gonna love it tonight." So far I haven't seen anyone under eighty.

Only one critic has arrived—my waiting, ticketless friend—when Irving asks me, "Who's here so far?"

I say, "Well, I saw your wife, Fanny, Paulette Goddard with Earl Blackwell, Adolph Green and Phyllis Newman, Leonard and Felicia Bernstein, David Merrick, Alex and Hildy Cohen, and Andy Warhol."

He seems annoyed. "I've seen them, too. What about the critics?"

"Don't worry. They'll be here. That's what they get paid for."

Harry arrives with the press list. I personally escort the ticketless critic and his wife into the theatre and down the aisle to their seats. Two elderly ladies are sitting in them.

I politely ask, "May I please see your stubs?"

One of the ladies hands them to me. They are the tickets that had been sent to the critic. I wonder how she acquired them, and she tells me that her son gave them to her as a present. I then learn that her loving son is a copyboy at the critic's newspaper. I tell her she's in the wrong seats and ask her to come with me. I have the box office punch up two unsold balcony seats and give them to her. I do not have the heart to tell her that her son may be a sneak thief. Either he is being kind to his mother by sending her to the theatre, or he is trying to frame her.

More people enter the theatre. Some are genuine celebrities, others pose as them. Most are formally dressed. A few, though, are wearing turtlenecks and jeans, with large, gold-plated medallions hanging from heavy chains around their necks. There are too many bouffant hairdos in the audience. Too many mink coats. I am seized with a severe case of opening-night paranoia. All of them are out to get me. I just know it.

It is 6:55. The critics begin to arrive. Clive Barnes of the *Times* smiles and says, "Call me at 11:00."

Richard Watts of the *Post* smiles and says, "Call me at midnight."

Doug Watt of the *News* smiles and says, "Howya doing, Harvey?"

John Simon of *New York Magazine* arrives scowling, even though he is accompanied by a stunning girl.

The key critics are all in the house now. I advise Irving to tell the stage manager to go, and I take my seat next to Sarah on the aisle in the last row. The house lights go down, the curtain rises, and the play begins.

It is impossible for me to concentrate on the stage action. I spend most of the first act studying the audience. They are giggling controllably. I strain to see how the critics are reacting. All I can make out are the backs of their heads. In exactly forty-two minutes, the first act ends and the house lights come up again. The audience strolls up the aisle for a smoke, a stretch, a visit to the lounge, or merely to be seen. Because it is raining, they crowd the back of the house and the lobby. Clouds of smoke envelop these huddled masses yearning to breathe free. I am the target of such remarks as "It's going well, isn't it?" or "It's a very pleasant evening in the theatre."

No longer able to face such withering attacks, I seek refuge backstage. There I find Gannon, Worth, and Martin. Gannon says, "The first act never played better."

Worth says, "It's not playing like it did last night. The audience is not reacting."

Martin says, "We could have used two more weeks out of town."

I say, "I wonder who the Knicks are playing tonight?"

The stage manager says, "Second act places, please."

That is my cue to return to my seat for the second spasm of the same fit. My wife asks, "How do you think it's going?"

I reply, "I can't tell. What did you hear during the intermission?"

"They weren't talking about the play. Everything but. Do you have a mint or a piece of gum?"

The second act goes well. Natalie's bikini gets an ovation. If she had appeared nude, I think she'd have gotten a standing ovation.

During the second intermission I take my wife to the bar across the street and we have double Frescas, straight up.

Throughout the third act I strain my eyes trying to read the program biographies with the help of a pencil flashlight. Harry has written them forthrightly. In no way do they equal in interest a railroad timetable. I discover that Philip Carlisle is his real name, that he attended the Princeton Country Day School, made his Broadway stage debut as a sailor in *Mister Roberts*, and last appeared on the screen in *The Cruel Range*, a Western made in Spain.

I whisper to my wife, "When the curtain falls, you go directly to Sardi's with the Ashes. Order me a Spanish omelet. I'll be right over as soon as I finish taking pictures backstage."

I return to my *Playbill*, but before I can read the restaurant column, the play ends. The critics dash madly up the aisle, tripping over their coats. Half a dozen have tight deadlines; the others have Pavlovian reactions and follow, lest they be forced to remain in their seats and applaud what they have seen. I try to read their faces, but they reveal little more than the desperate urge to leave the building. There are five wildly enthusiastic curtain calls, ignited by seventy-five backers who have been warned by Gannon that a display of emotion will influence the critics and insure the return of their investments. Not one critic has remained for the curtain calls.

Sarah heads for Sardi's and I beat my way backstage. The pushing and shoving compares with that of the Tokyo subway at rush hour. Hordes of well-wishers block my path, but I cross the goal line, winning icy stares or vile epithets in the process. I must reach Natalie's dressing room before Harry arrives with the photographers.

Natalie is surrounded by friends and enemies. They take turns saying, "Darling, you were wonderful. It's going to be a great success." A great deal of asexual kissing is going on.

Harry arrives with two worn-out photographers in rumpled suits. "Go to Phil's dressing room and ask him to come here to pose for pictures," I tell him. "And bring up Gannon, Worth, and Martin."

Natalie spots me out of the corner of her eye. "How do you think it went?" she asks.

"Very well. You were wonderful." She smiles gratefully.

Harry returns. He tells me that Philip is balking. He wants Natalie to come to *his* dressing room. The others are on the way. "To hell with Philip," I mutter. "We don't need him anyway."

Gannon pushes his way into the room. He grabs my arm tightly and asks, "Have you heard anything yet?" I shake my head. Worth and Martin arrive, followed by Philip in a green silk dressing gown and ascot. All of them peck Natalie on the cheek and tell her, "Darling, you were wonderful."

I line them up for photos. Their faces are beaming as flashbulbs pop. With every click of the shutter, the smiles disappear. Five times the photographers shout, "Just one more, please."

"That's it," I tell them, and we all leave the dressing room. As I buck the crowds again, a woman with Dracula-like eye makeup and overpowering perfume grabs and kisses me, shrieking, "Darling, you were wonderful."

I struggle to reach the street. An autograph hound with his album open and a pen in his hand runs up to me, stares at my face, and says, "Aw, you're nobody."

The night air revives me, and all alone at last, I walk over to Sardi's. My wife has ordered me a club steak. "What about the Spanish omelet?" I ask. She reminds me, "You had eggs for breakfast."

Ingram says, "It's not going to be a fun evening. I hated the show. It hasn't got a chance."

"You're probably right," I say, "but we've worked on worse. You never can tell. Remember *Any Wednesday?* We just about gave up on that one and it ran two years. It's been a lousy season. Maybe they'll go easy on this one."

We make small talk about past European vacations while we eat. Natalie and Philip enter Sardi's for the obligatory wave of applause before going to the opening-night party. The applause is led by Martin, the headwaiter, who has not seen the show. Ten people ask me if I've heard anything yet.

It is time to go up to Ingram's office, which is on the seventh floor of the Sardi Building. In the conference room is a battery of four television sets arranged on the shelf of a wall unit. We tune in the Channel Five news in time to learn that the Knicks have lost to the Chicago Bulls in overtime.

It is peaceful until the elevator deposits Gannon, Worth, Martin, and a dozen camp followers on the seventh floor. They invade the conference room. Gannon asks, "Have you heard anything yet? When does that jerk Klein go on?"

We assume that most of this well-dressed mob are backers, friends, and mistresses, past and present, of our esteemed producer. The cleavage is deep, the jewelry flashy, the hair well teased and firmly sprayed, the conversation desultory. Several of these theatre lovers demand, "Where's the Scotch? Isn't there anything to drink in this damned office?" Others insist on knowing where they are, which is encouraging, since inquisitiveness is one of the first signs of the growing child's developing intellect. Ingram sacrifices a fifth of his best Scotch to his new-found friends, who now request potato chips.

I glance at the TV sets. Stewart Klein is on, on all four, but I cannot hear him over the din. "Shut up, everybody. Channel Five is on."

They quiet down, and we hear Klein say " . . . *The Crux* is wafer thin, but if you enjoy light confections, there are moments that will make you chuckle. I did from time to time. This is Stewart Klein for Channel Five news."

The group begins to cheer. Gannon yells above the roar, "He loved it. Did you hear that? He loved it. He's an astute critic. He knew exactly what we were trying to do."

I look at my notes and the only words of Klein that I have written down are "wafer," "confection," and "chuckle." It sounds as though he has reviewed a Fanny Farmer shop.

At 11:10, I sneak out of the conference room and into an empty office to call my friend at the *Times*. "Harvey? Ah, yes, hold it a moment," Clive says. I figure he has to pull out his notice of *The Crux* from a pile that also includes reviews of a ballet and an off-off-Broadway play, all written within the last hour and a half. "Here it is," he says jovially, and begins to read: "*The Crux* is the kind of play that Broadway audiences used to adore. It has a beginning, a middle, and an end, but it is as thin as a shadow. It deals with a marriage gone sour when the wife decides she wants to grow up to be Gloria Steinem. A fair premise for a light comedy . . . "

Barnes continues reading and I make notes as fast as I can. His review winds up, "*The Crux* is at best mildly diverting. I neither hated nor adored it. If you care at all for wispy boulevard comedy, it might be your cup of tea."

"Thank you, Clive," I say.

"What do you think?" he asks.

"It's a fair appraisal. I agree with you. Good night and love to Trish."

I decide to call Doug Watt at the *News* before returning to the conference room. "How did you like it, Doug?" I ask.

"I wouldn't say I liked it," he replies. "I didn't hate it either. My review will be mixed."

We say goodnight to each other, and I return to the revelers. They are watching Leonard Harris on Channel Two. They're all talking at the same time and I can't hear a word he's saying. My wife is sitting next to the TV sets, and she tells me that she thinks his review is both good and bad.

I report the key points of Barnes's review to Gannon. His joy is unbridled. He shouts, "Shut up, everybody. Barnes loves the show. We're in. We're a smash."

I relay Watt's comment and he is positively euphoric. I obviously haven't made a single thing clear.

At midnight I phone Dick Watts. Before I can get a word out, he says, "Hello, Harvey, I recognized your ring. I didn't think it was too bad. It's a pleasant show and although I have reservations, my notice will not be negative."

From another room somebody yells that Kevin Sanders of Channel Seven has just panned the show. "He doesn't count," remarks the triumphant Gannon. "Let's go to the party and celebrate."

I beg off by telling him that tomorrow is going to be such a busy day that I better get some rest. He calls me a party-pooper.

As they leave, the playwright takes me aside and whispers, "Is it really a hit, or is Gannon acting out a fantasy?"

"It'll be a struggle," I tell him. "We're living in hard times. Have a good time at the party, but wait a few days before you buy a house in East Hampton."

We're alone again, just the four of us. We recap the evening. "Gannon really believes he has a hit," says Ingram. "Wait until tomorrow morning when he doesn't see a soul at the box office. How can a man delude himself so?"

"It's easy in our business," I say. "You set yourself up for the worst. You expect to get killed and when it doesn't turn out all that bad, you're just ecstatic with relief."

At nine dollars for an orchestra seat, *The Crux* is not exactly a bargain. The public has a sixth sense about these things, and my experience tells me that it will probably peter out in a few weeks, perhaps as early as next Saturday.

My wife and I say goodnight, pick up our car, and head home. On the way I tell her, "I dread tomorrow. Nothing I can do will save this show. And when it closes, they'll blame me for its failure."

"You're not personally responsible," she answers me. "It's really a terrible play, so don't kill yourself, because it won't help. Where did you get that ridiculous bow tie? I just noticed it."

"Don't laugh," I say. "I'm planning to hang myself with it."

"I never heard of anybody hanging himself with a clip-on bow tie. You know what? You're in a terrible business, and it's making you crazy."

As we open the front door, the phone is ringing. It is Gannon. "You're missing a great party, Harvey, baby. I just wanted to thank you for what you did tonight. Get a good night's sleep, 'cause starting tomorrow, it's up to you."

I go to the medicine cabinet and take one Valium and one Seconal. I undress, wash, and go to bed. In the night I have this horrible nightmare. I am riding in the subway with my neighbor, and he turns to me and says, "Of all the people I know, you have the most interesting job."

7
Ad Nauseam

The clock-radio goes on at 7:15 Friday morning. I awake to the intense voice of a newscaster. After headlines about war, peace, shortages, inflation, chicanery in high places, strikes, murder, pollution, sports, and the weather, he shifts vocal gears: "Last night a new play opened at the Plymouth Theatre and today the whole town is talking about it. It's called *The Crux,* and it stars two of Hollywood's greatest names, Natalie Borden and Philip Carlisle. *The Crux* will provide you with one of the most exciting evenings in the theatre in years. It's a play that could be about you, me, or the people next door. It's as timely as today's headlines and as refreshing as a glass of sparkling champagne. Take our advice. Rush to the Plymouth Theatre and get your tickets today for *The Crux.* Don't miss it."

My wife rolls over and says, "That's one good notice at least."

"The hell it is," I say. "That's a paid commercial. I wrote it five days ago."

"Lousy huckster," she says. "Do people really believe that crap?"

"You did."

"I'm half asleep and totally exhausted. What time is it?"

"Twenty after seven," I say.

"Go back to sleep. How will you get through the day on five hours sleep?"

"I wish I'd had five hours," I say. "I must have spent two just tossing, trying to lay out an ad campaign for *The Crux*. I hate shows that are neither hits nor flops."

"So does the public," she says. "Go back to sleep or go downtown, but stop talking to me and keeping me awake. And next time, don't set the clock-radio after a late night."

"I didn't. I forgot to turn it off yesterday."

I dress, tiptoe downstairs, open the front door, and look for my *Times* and *News*. I want to read, from beginning to end, the Barnes and Watt reviews. The papers aren't there. Damn that son of a bitch. I pay my bills on time. Why can't he deliver them on time?

I hear my wife coming down the stairs. "I can't sleep," she says. "Let me make you some breakfast. How will you be able to write more of those deceitful commercials on an empty stomach?"

"I'm not hungry and I'm mad as hell," I reply, "The papers aren't here yet."

"Did you look up in the tree? Sometimes his aim is bad."

The papers are up in the tree all right, resting on a high branch. I bring a stepladder from the kitchen and start to climb. My wife tries to be helpful. "Here, let me hold it steady for you. In your condition, you could fall and break an ankle."

"It should only happen," I say. "Then I wouldn't have to go into the city and bullshit my way through that ad meeting. The show could close and it wouldn't be my fault."

"I already told you, it won't be your fault. Only Gannon and his stooges will blame you. They won't blame themselves for putting on such a rotten play."

A quick glance at the front page of the *Times* adds to my depression. Only horror stalked the planet yesterday. Nor do the sports pages buoy my spirits as I read how the Knicks blew last night's game.

Setting a cup of bland decaffeinated coffee before me, my wife asks, "How does the review look in print?"

"I haven't gotten to it yet," I reply. "Isn't it more important to see what's going on in the world first?"

"Your world begins at Forty-fourth Street and ends at Forty-ninth Street," she says.

I turn to the theatre page and read Barnes's notice. The headline is hardly inspiring: "Diverting *Crux* Opens at Plymouth." The review itself doesn't read as well as it sounded last night when I heard it over the phone. "It won't sell a ticket, sweetie," I say. "Squeezing a quote out of it will give me a hernia."

"But you're so good at putting together those quote ads," she reminds me. "The problem is that nobody believes them anymore. I never even bother to read them."

"You got a better idea?" I ask.

"Yes, tell Gannon to close the show tomorrow night and return what money is left to his backers."

The *News* review is equally unenthusiastic. Although it is not an outright pan, it is liberally sprinkled with words like "pap," "routine," and "lifeless." "The only thing I can quote from this one is a line about the cast," I say. "It claims they're all 'pleasant.' That's terrific. How many pleasant people can you find in the world today?"

My wife answers, "You *used* to be pleasant. I'm going back to sleep now. Don't work too hard today."

I yell after her, "What does that mean? 'Don't work too hard today'? If you think that pushing a ton of garbage like *The Crux* isn't hard work, you're crazy."

At the newsstand near the subway entrance, I pick up copies of *Newsday,* the *Long Island Press,* and the *Journal of Commerce.* They all agree on two things: gasoline prices are going up and *The Crux* isn't much of a show.

My first stop in Manhattan is the Plymouth. Although I know the answer, I want to see for myself if anyone is foolish enough to come to the box office for tickets at 9:30 in the morning. Nobody is there except the porter, who is mopping the lobby floor. "Anybody been here yet this morning?" I ask him.

"Didn't see a soul," he says. "This show's in big trouble. I can tell. If it's a hit, people take their programs home with them. I been picking up a lot of programs this morning."

I walked through a deserted Shubert Alley. Puddles of rainwater are beginning to evaporate in the morning sun, but there is still a damp chill in the air. Not bloody likely that anyone will venture out this morning to buy tickets for anything, let alone *The Crux.*

"How'd the show go last night?" asks George, the elevator operator in the Sardi Building.

"Only fair," I tell him.

"It's up to you," he says.

Ingram is all alone in his office. He is reading the morning papers. "I can't see how we can put together a quote ad out of these," he says, pushing them aside. "Anybody at the box office?"

"There's a line around the block . . . at Radio City Music Hall," I snap back.

"Up yours. Boy, am I exhausted. I took a room at the Piccadilly and never closed my eyes. I gave up trying at 3:15, turned on the TV, and watched Wallace Beery in *Viva Villa.* It's a damn good picture. Think I'll go to Mexico this summer."

Ingram also has all the transcripts of the radio and television reviews on his desk. I give each one a cursory reading. If nothing else, they're consistent. They all contain little goodies of praise, which are counteracted by words of harsh criticism.

"What about the AP and UPI?" I ask.

"The same," he replies. "You know, nobody really went all out for the show, but nobody killed it outright."

"Yes, Kevin Sanders on Channel Seven did."

"He doesn't count, according to Gannon. Say, when is the great producer coming up?"

"I told him 10:00. He should be here any minute, so let's

at least organize our ideas before he arrives."

We discuss the advisability of a large quote ad and reject it because there just aren't enough good words to justify the expenditure. "What about a full-page ad with no quotes and just a lot of white space?" I ask. "We can print a public service message at the top, 'This ad is brought to you by *The Crux*. To conserve paper, please use our complimentary white space for phone messages, shopping lists, or doodling.'"

"It's original," says Ingram unenthusiastically, "but with no advance sale and wishy-washy notices, the best thing we can do is continue the current radio campaign. Do they have any money left for promotion?"

"Probably zilch. They took a terrible beating out of town. We'll ask when he gets here."

We kick around other ideas, such as TV spots, subway posters, billboards along the main auto routes, and dismiss them all as either too costly or too long-range to be of immediate benefit. It seems strange that between the two of us, with fifty years of combined experience, we cannot cope with the particular problem presented by *The Crux*.

I have always known that a press agent is only as good as the show he is selling. There was a time when a play with mixed notices could be made to run for a while, even to the point of being profitable, but inflated ticket prices, competitive entertainment, and high operating costs have made this virtually impossible.

I ask Ingram, "Aren't there times when you wish you were in product advertising? After analyzing the market, you'd know where you want to go, and you'd have the preplanned budgets to take you there. You wouldn't have to worry about reviews or the inability to set up a proper campaign until after the opening. You'd be able to film decent TV commercials and tape clever radio spots. Wouldn't it be wonderful?"

He shrugs, and replies, "I don't know. The theatre is the most interesting job in the world. You get to go to opening nights. You meet all the stars. What's more exciting than theatre?"

"Professional basketball," I tell him.

We hear footsteps out in the hallway. It's Gannon, accompanied by an entourage. He shouts, "Where the hell are you guys?"

We yell back, "In here where you left us last night."

Gannon is escorted by Irving, Jerry, Kevin, his latest girl friend, Iris, and his son, Tony, aged nineteen. I am delighted that he has brought a panel of experts with him. He is still basking in the glow of the opening. "You should have been there last night," he says. "What a party! Hey, we just passed the Plymouth and there are two people in line."

Ingram and I look at each other in dismay. Before it is too late, I must make an effort to bring him back to earth.

"That was ten minutes ago," I tell him. "What's it like now?"

Gannon instructs Irving to call the box office for a more up-to-date reading. I ask Tony if he was at the opening. "No," he replies, "I saw it in Boston. A friend took me to a rock concert at Madison Square Garden last night."

I like the boy immediately. He has taste and judgment. Gannon should be proud of him. He is everything his father will never grow up to be.

Gannon demands some coffee, and calls the meeting to order. "The way I figure it," he says, "we've got enough quotes for a full-page ad next Monday and the following Sunday in the *Times*. On the top we say, 'The Broadway Season's First Blockbuster.' I've been playing around with the quotes. Listen to what I've gotten out of Barnes. 'Diverting. It might be your cup of tea.' "

I interrupt. "He said 'mildly diverting.' "

"Aw, c'mon," says Gannon, "he wouldn't mind a little thing like omitting 'mildly.' And if he does, it'll be too late. The ad will already have run."

He continues, "From Doug Watt, I have 'a pleasant company is headed by the still attractive Natalie Borden and the upstanding Philip Carlisle.' Now don't tell me you guys can't get equally good stuff from the other notices."

Irving has spoken to the box office "There's nobody

there now," he says, "but the phones are ringing."

For more than a quarter of a century, I have heard that remark from veteran managers, producers, and box office men. "The phones are ringing." By now I understand it means only that ticket brokers are calling to see if they can return their allotments. Or people who have bought tickets for next week want to know if the show will run that long.

"The action won't start until the lunch hour," claims the optimistic Gannon. "Besides, today's Friday. People get paid today."

His point eludes me completely. A sure-fire hit shows its true colors early. Neither snow, rain, sleet, nor gloom of night will deter the eager ticket buyer if he really wants to buy. A line of fifteen people when I passed the Plymouth earlier would have started my heart beating. Now, Gannon's self-delusion only depresses me. He truly believes that we can pull together twelve to fifteen quotes, the very least needed for a full-page ad. He not only wants to run the ad in the *Times*, but in the *News, Post,* and *Women's Wear Daily* as well. "So much for the quote ads," he says. "What do you guys think about radio?"

"Now you're talking," answers Ingram. "We can either continue our present spots or do new ones. If we could get your stars together this afternoon, we could have them tape some and have them on the air tonight. Radio is the best answer. By the time the newspaper ads appear, three days will have passed."

Gannon asks how much it will all cost him and Ingram does hasty calculations. It comes to approximately $35,000. Gannon hardly blinks at this figure. Up to now no one among his camp followers has spoken. Suddenly Iris pipes up in a shrill voice, "Can't you get Philip on the Johnny Carson show this evening?"

I coolly tell her, "That could be a little difficult. The Carson show comes from the West Coast. Tonight's show was taped yesterday. And who knows if Carson wants him in the first place."

"Wait a minute," cries Gannon. "Don't put her down.

It's not such a bad idea. I'll buy the fact that you can't get him on tonight. But what about Monday? We'll cancel the Monday performance and fly Philip out. It's worth it for the plug. You can also put Natalie on the 'Today' show Monday morning. She won't mind getting up at six. She did it for years in Hollywood making pictures.

"C'mon, baby, this is no time to quit on me. Can't you have the daily *Times* interview one of them over the weekend, and the Sunday *Times* do the other one at the same time? And what about Jerry here? I'm sure Rex Reed would do him. I could call Rex myself. Didn't Barnes say that Jerry's one of our finest writers of boulevard comedy. Didn't he?"

"No, he didn't," I say, "but I'll try. Believe me, I'll try."

Gannon turns to Irving. "How much money do we have left in the till?"

Irving answers, "About five thousand, not including bonds posted with the unions. We owe about ten thousand in unpaid bills and the show breaks even at thirty-five thousand a week. Don't you think we ought to give it a few days before spending all that money on advertising?"

"Hell, no," shouts Gannon. "If I looked at it that way, I'd close tomorrow night. Let's cut everything else down to the bone. I'm sure Jerry will slice his royalties. Right, Jerry?"

Jerry purses his lips but doesn't answer. Gannon continues. "Certainly the actors will take salary cuts. Ask everybody to cooperate. I'll even trim my office expenses."

He bangs his hand on Ingram's desk and says, "I just know that this is an audience show and no matter what the critics say, we can run and be a hit. Now you guys start putting the ads together. I'm going over to ask the Shuberts to chip in. They don't want a dark house on their hands. Maybe they'll pay for part of the advertising. They like me, and they know I'm a fighter."

Gannon realizes he has uttered the perfect exit line. He and his business advisors leave. Ingram looks worried. He knows that if he runs the ads as ordered, he may never be paid for them. At the same time, he doesn't want to be responsible for forcing a decision to close. My stake is somewhat smaller. I want the show to run because it pays me a salary every week it does. At the same time, I don't want to see anyone killed financially. Gannon's responsibility is even greater. If the total cost of the production exceeds the capital he originally raised, he will be personally liable for every additional penny. I hate myself for not being entirely honest, for not telling him that any quote ad we can squeeze out of the reviews is beyond credibility and won't work anyway.

"Stop beating yourself," Ingram says. "This isn't Gannon's first show. He's been around a while. Look at all he knows about advertising and promotion. He's even a friend of Rex Reed."

We spend the rest of the morning working on the ad. By liberal use of photographs, we manage to cut down on the space for the quotes themselves. By lunch time, we have come up with a layout that seems almost plausible, without misquoting a single reviewer. We decide to break for lunch and check the Plymouth box office. The lobby is still empty. The treasurer is reading the *Times*. Without looking up, he asks, "How many, please?"

"Fifty orchestra seats for tonight's performance, on the side and in the rear," I say, startling him out of his concentration on the stock market listings.

"Oh, it's you," he says. "Are they gonna run? So far I've sold maybe twenty, twenty-five tickets. But the phones are ringing."

"Gannon is determined to run," I tell him. "He's out raising more money right now."

"I hope he gets it, for your sake," he says.

"For that remark," I say, "I hereby sentence you to watch the play for the next ten performances."

"That'll be the day. I haven't seen a show since I started working here seven years ago."

Ingram and I lunch on tongue sandwiches and coleslaw at the Gaiety Delicatessen, then go our separate ways—he to work with his staff on the mechanical production of the ad, I to try to put together some semblance of a publicity campaign.

Rex Reed tells me he didn't mind *The Crux* too much. He has no interest in interviewing Jerry, who happens to be an old friend of his, and "a terrible bore who never opens his mouth." He says he'd prefer to interview Natalie, but has to do Goldie Hawn, Jack Nicholson, Mia Farrow, and Jon Voight before he could possibly get to her. He promises to call me in a month. Nice guy, Rex Reed. Just can't say no.

The cultural editor of the daily *Times* says, "Let's wait and see what the Sunday edition is planning. As soon as I hear, I'll call you."

I put in a long distance call to Johnny Carson's producer. He's happy to hear from me until I tell him why I'm calling. "Borden and Carlisle are has-beens," he says. "Besides, Johnny's going on vacation and Shecky Greene is taking over. Can you just picture either of your stiffs with Shecky Greene?"

The producer of the "Today" show promises to use both my stars if he ever does a show on "Hollywood in the Fifties."

I call Earl Wilson. "Earl, you know that bikini Natalie Borden wears in *The Crux*? Well, it cost five hundred bucks to make. Yeah, no kidding, Earl. Would I steer you wrong? How about an interview with Natalie? Sure, I'll call you in ten days."

My secretary comes up with a suggestion. "Why don't you try to put Miss Borden and Mr. Carlisle on 'Face the Nation'? They could give advice to struggling young actors and drama students. It would be such a relief from all those crooked politicians."

Harry, my trusty aide, makes a contribution. "What about the 'Million Dollar Movie' doing a Borden-Carlisle film festival over the next few weeks? She once received an Oscar nomination for her performance as an American tourist in *It Happened One Afternoon in Barcelona*. Remember that one?"

The afternoon is not a total loss. By four we are able to set interviews with three local radio shows, two TV shows, and newspapers in Bergen County (Kevin Martin was born there), Newark (Gannon was raised there), and Westport (Jerry Worth lives there). The *Wall Street Journal* wants to profile Gannon. The angle? How he prepared for the legitimate theatre by becoming a real estate syndicator.

Ingram advises me that he'll have the full-page ad ready to show at 7:00 tonight. I tell him, "Let's meet at the Plymouth and we'll get Gannon to okay it. It's a lot of money, and I don't want the responsibility."

Repeated checks with the box office reveal that business has not improved during the day. The lunch hour landslide predicted by Gannon has not materialized. Meanwhile my phones are bombarded with calls from "friends" in the business who would like to see the show tonight for free. I think, why not take care of them? It's better than having the actors play to upholstered seats.

Gannon calls. "You know what's going to make this show?" he says. "Mouth-to-mouth."

"In the end that's what makes every show, Daniel," I say. "Mouth-to-mouth is bigger than you and me. It's even bigger than word-of-mouth."

"Yeah, that's right," he says. "Have you heard about the national magazines and Walter Kerr yet?"

"*Time* is doing us a favor. They're not running a review, which is a break, since their critic didn't care for it. I can't reach anyone at *Newsweek*. Kerr hasn't written his yet. And John Simon says he was under the impression that Natalie was wearing a body stocking under her bikini and that it had a hole in the toe."

"Why does that Simon have to be so nasty? You know, someday I'm gonna have one of my ex-partners put out a contract on him."

I suddenly find myself in the peculiar position of pleading for John Simon's life. "I'm only kidding," he says. "Let's meet backstage at the Plymouth at 7:15 tonight."

The second-night performance of most Broadway shows, particularly those that are not out-and-out hits, is the greatest anticlimax since premature ejaculation. A good many of the orchestra seats are occupied by those representatives of the press who are not considered important enough to attend the opening, or who have manageable egos. If I were a journalist, I would much prefer to be on the second-night press list. It affords the opportunity of reading the notices first and, if the play sounds unappetizing, of coming up with an acceptable excuse for not attending. For those without conscience, excuses aren't necessary. They merely give their tickets to someone in the sports department in return for future favors, or throw them away without calling the press agent.

One of the few benefits afforded by second nights is the total absence of tension. In most cases the die is cast, or the cast is dying. This time I am the perfect social butterfly, welcoming old friends into my theatre. Virtually everybody on the second-night press list will be receiving a call from me on Monday, requesting they do something for *The Crux*. Now is the time to turn on the charm.

"I hope you enjoy it," I say to everyone.

"I never read the notices anyway," says a female writer for a monthly magazine. Her tone belies her statement. She has probably read every one.

A rival producer passes me in the lobby. He says, "I wanted to catch it before it closes. I hear the costume designer is talented."

My cousin and his wife, whom I have invited, stop to chat. "Do you think you can get us tickets to a Knicks playoff game?" he asks. "I wouldn't be caught dead here tonight if it weren't for her. Now she owes me one."

A photo editor corners me. "My wife, Flossie, here, and I love the theatre," he says. "We've seen everything on and off-Broadway this season, and this summer we're going on a theatre tour of London. Seven shows in seven nights. Anything you can recommend there?"

I tell him, "Don't miss the Old Vic and the Young Vic," and wonder why they haven't got a Middle-aged Vic.

These fifteen endless minutes having illuminated my

life, I drift backstage to the empty dressing room where Gannon is sitting. Ingram is waiting at the door, the full-page ad in a large gray envelope. The producer looks worn and dejected. "Let me see it," he says.

The ad is a beautiful piece of work. It tells its story clearly and tastefully. If the show itself were only as good as the ad, I reflect. "I like it," says Gannon. "Let me take it to Natalie and Philip. You guys wait here."

He returns a few minutes later. "They were impressed. But don't run it until you hear from me tomorrow," he says to us. "We took in only fifteen hundred dollars today. I'm still waiting for word from the Shuberts, the actors' agents, the playwright, and the director. I've asked them all to take cuts. If they want this show to run, they'll have to cooperate. There's nothing in it for me now, outside of a possible picture sale. It's up to them."

Thank heavens it's no longer up to me. Now that the end may be in sight, I experience a sense of relief rather than sadness. "I hope they come through, Danny," I tell him, but I really don't mean it.

We say goodnight to each other and I head for the subway. On the way I am accosted by a panhandler asking for a quarter. Bet he used to be a producer. When I reach the house, Sarah asks me, "What kind of day did you have?"

"Oh, the usual," I reply.

Gannon is on my phone late the following afternoon. "I've just put up the notice," he says. "We close tonight. Kill everything."

"Wouldn't anybody come across?" I ask.

"Not in the way I wanted them to. Natalie's agent says they want her for a bus-and-truck company of *Irene*. Philip's agent says he can get him another spaghetti western now that he's back in the public eye. The Shuberts will help, but only up to a point. And Jerry says that Alex Cohen has just bought his new play and it wouldn't help his career to have this show hanging around for a while "

"I'm sorry, Daniel," I say with a catch in my voice, play' ing the sympathetic friend to the hilt.

"It wasn't your fault," he says, and hangs up.

I sit down at the typewriter and start to write the final release. "*The Crux* closed last Saturday night at the Plymouth, after four performances. The play, a modern tragedy by Jerome Worth . . . "

Yes, I tell myself, the playwright must really have known something when he called *The Crux* a "modern tragedy."

8

Lowlights of a Theatrical Career

No one is proud of failure, but assemble a group of theatre people and inevitably we will attempt to outdo each other with tales of calamity, large and small, encountered along the rutted routes we travel. Some masochistic streak within us enables us to wallow delightedly in the painful memories of disaster and disappointment. It amazes us when we emerge from these crises, if no wiser, at least in a reasonable state of well-being. A transatlantic voyage on the France was a lovely way to cross. But to have survived the sinking of the Titanic provides conversation fodder for the rest of one's days.

Those happy moments of triumph, when everything seems to go swimmingly, are few and far between in the theatre. Most of the time chaos is the norm. In his daily telephone calls to me, my client David Merrick would usually initiate the conversation by inquiring, "What fell apart?" Such fervent pessimism deserved its rewards. Invariably something had fallen apart, thereby providing us a common ground for discussion.

The word "trouble" is not overused in the theatre. Tell a colleague, "We're in trouble," and he knows immediately what you mean. George S. Kaufman once defined trouble as something that comes in a large box, and will surely be waiting for you in your Philadelphia hotel room when you arrive for the beginning of a pre-Broadway tryout.

In virtually every season of my career as a theatrical publicist, I was witness to or participant in a fair share of trouble. If you hang around long enough, you cannot escape. There were highlights, of course, but they were far outnumbered by the lowlights, which tend to lodge themselves in the brain, becoming more ridiculous with the passing of years. At the time they occurred, it seemed as if the world was coming to an end. When it didn't, we were completely surprised.

Beware of Hungarian Playwrights and Sons of Presidents

The Play's the Thing is a comedy by the famed playwright Ferenc Molnar, who wrote the more popular *Liliom*, Rodgers and Hammerstein's source material for the musical, *Carousel*. An English version of *The Play's the Thing*, adapted "from the Hungarian" by no less than P. G. Wodehouse, was presented during the 1947-48 season with Louis Calhern as the dashing writer, Sandor Turai, and Faye Emerson (Mrs. Elliott Roosevelt at the time), as a woman whose amorous past merited concealment from her fiancé, a young associate of Turai's.

We opened a pre-Broadway tryout in New Haven on a stifling night in early spring. The Shubert Theatre was not air-conditioned, and to ease the suffering of cast and audience, all theatre doors were left open, the traffic noises outside notwithstanding. The play was set in "a room in a castle on the Italian Riviera." Upstage center was a pair of magnificent French doors leading onto an Italian garden.

Deftly waving an ivory cigarette holder and striding back and forth across the stage, the suave and sophisticated Calhern, impeccable in white tie and tails, was delivering his major second-act speech, when in through the garden doors flew a bat. The audience was stirred, some to gasps of wonderment at this spontaneous but effective piece of realism, the rest to hysteria. I personally leaned toward the "realism" theory, since the play was by a Hungarian, and how close can you get to Transylvania without getting bitten on the neck? Maybe this was the director's inspiration.

Then I noticed the shock that contorted Calhern's features as the bat kept pace with him. He dodged, he ducked, he swerved. He took every measure possible to avoid a head-on collision with the flying rodent. But great actor that he was, he never missed a line.

Satisfied that its stage debut had been a startling success, the bat flew out the garden doors. And with it flew the play, which was never sufficiently exciting to recapture the audience's attention.

We moved to Washington for an engagement at the National Theatre. The critics there were constructive. They rebuked the production because its pace was too slow. In desperation, the coproducers, James Russo and Michael Ellis, called Molnar in New York. Neither he nor Wodehouse had joined the play's pre-Broadway meanderings. They reached him at his favorite afternoon haunt, Rumpelmayer's, in the St. Moritz Hotel, where he stopped for daily tea and a sweet. On hearing that the reviewers had rapped his play because it was slow-moving, he advised, "Tell the actors to talk faster."

With accelerated dialogue, *The Play's the Thing* settled into the Booth Theatre on Shubert Alley for a modest run. My boss, Sam Friedman, hired an associate publicist, Abner Klipstein, who, at five-one, was, and still is, the shortest male member of the Association of Theatrical Press Agents and Managers. Sam and I brought Abner to the Booth to introduce him to the cast. I waited outside

Faye Emerson's tiny dressing room while Sam and Abner entered. Elliott Roosevelt was present, too, having taken an active interest in his wife's career. He began to offer a detailed critique of Sam's approach to Miss Emerson's publicity, a dangerous tactic in dealing with one as volatile as Sam Friedman. Winding up like some grotesque curveball pitcher, Sam took a swing at Roosevelt, who ducked. Abner took the punch squarely on the jaw, and came reeling out the dressing-room door, landing on the corridor floor. I cradled his half-conscious body, and comforted him. He looked up at me, and gasped, "I never got to meet Faye Emerson."

Has There Ever Been a Hit about an Undertaker?

My brother Lee had made a large sum of money producing *Finian's Rainbow*, and had rented a spacious home in New Milford, Connecticut, for the summer. On an unbearably hot night in August, he took pity on my wife and me and invited us to spend the weekend. We happily accepted, and took the New Haven Railroad to New Milford, where Lee picked us up and drove us to his house. He told us that his other weekend guests were the eminent producer-director, Herman Shumlin, and his wife. He explained that he had found a new play, for which Shumlin shared his enthusiasm, and had agreed to direct. I was impressed. Lee wanted me to read the script before retiring, and to discuss it with him at breakfast.

After refreshing ourselves with glasses of iced tea, Sarah and I took the script to our bedroom and read it. It was titled *The Biggest Thief in Town*, and had been written by Dalton Trumbo, a topflight scenarist who had turned out major motion pictures, as well as a searing novel, *Johnny Got His Gun*, about a World War I basket case.

The Biggest Thief in Town related the misadventures of an undertaker in a small Colorado community. He waits for the rich man, who lives in the castle on the hill overlooking the town, to die. When the happy moment comes, he intends to be the first mortician on the scene, snatch the body, and arrange an expensive funeral, the proceeds of which he will give to his daughter to enable her to escape her stultifying smalltown existence.

My wife and I agreed about the script. We did not care for it at all, and were unable to determine if it was intended as a serious play or a comedy-melodrama.

At breakfast the next morning, I was asked for my opinion, and being young and inexperienced at these things, offered it straight out. "What do *you* know?" said my brother, dismayed by my negative response. "Herman loves it, and we start rehearsals in mid-winter. Your opinion doesn't count."

Lee was right; I knew nothing. He had produced four shows and could be proud of every one. Shumlin had been a ranking director for eighteen years, and had staged such successes as *Grand Hotel, The Children's Hour, The Little Foxes, The Male Animal, The Corn Is Green,* and *Watch on the Rhine.* I had been toiling in the professional theatre for only eleven months.

With a cast that included Thomas Mitchell, Walter Abel, and Lois Nettleton, *The Biggest Thief in Town* opened at the Cort Theatre in late March of 1949. The critics couldn't decide whether it was a serious play or a comedy-melodrama. It closed after thirteen performances, but I did not have the *chutzpah* to say, "I told you so." It is easy, I realized, to become an expert in theatre by expressing negative opinions. The odds are always with you.

Shumlin went on to other triumphs. Trumbo was black-listed in Hollywood for his politics, but he continued to write films under assumed names, eventually regaining his identity with *Exodus,* when producer Otto Preminger had the courage to list him among the credits. But he never wrote another produced play. I almost made it to the unemployment insurance office, but for a small piece of luck.

A new comedy about army life had opened on Broadway just three weeks before *The Biggest Thief in Town.* Since

World War II was four years behind us, comedies about army life were now acceptable. There were ten million veterans who could laugh at these army-camp capers despite the shock of recognition. *At War with the Army* was by James B. Allardice, recently emerged from the Yale Drama School, where he had written the play. It was a nervous hit, whose prospects for long life were not clearcut yet. The show's press agent was Michel Mok, a former New York *Post* reporter, who was intelligent but insecure. Mok felt he could not give *At War with the Army* the imaginative, aggressive publicity campaign it required for survival. Besides, he was about to go to work for his prime clients, Rodgers and Hammerstein, who were preparing a new musical, to be called *South Pacific*.

The producers of *At War with the Army* sought outside help, and they engaged Sam Friedman, not a day too soon for my benefit. Sam did a fabulous job over the next few weeks. The show established itself, and bid fair to run through the summer and into the following season.

The producers thrived on Sam's counsel. They came to our office in early June to ask his advice regarding economic measures to sustain them during the July lull in box-office business. Honesty was Sam's strong suit. He told them how to cut expenses in various departments, and then made a dramatic suggestion. "Fire me," he said. "You're still obligated to pay Mok because he has a run-of-the-play contract. Having two press agents on the payroll is a strain."

"That's the last thing we'd do," they countered. "You're the guy responsible for getting us on our feet."

That night I made a routine visit to the Booth Theatre, where the show was playing. The company manager handed me an envelope for Sam. It contained his dismissal notice, along with a letter thanking him for his sage advice.

Allardice never wrote another Broadway play, and this time I made it to the unemployment office.

Enchanted to Meet You

The Enchanted excited me. For the first time in my burgeoning career, I was going to work on a George S. Kaufman-directed production. Other kids admired Joe DiMaggio; my idol was George Kaufman.

The Enchanted was a comedy, with overtones of fantasy, by the late French playwright Jean Giraudoux. A Broadway production of *Madwoman of Chaillot* had been running for a year in a graceful adaptation by Maurice Valency, a Columbia professor who also adapted *The Enchanted*.

Kaufman had recently married the attractive British actress Leueen MacGrath, who was to play the lead in *The Enchanted*, a young schoolteacher whose fantasy world brings happiness to a small, provincial French town. She is pursued by the town supervisor, but she becomes enamored of a gallant ghost who frequents her attic abode.

The music for the play had been composed by Francis Poulenc, the settings designed by Robert Edmond Jones, dean of scenic artists. All the elements were first rate. I could hardly wait for the first rehearsal when I would meet all the brilliant talents, but most particularly, George S. Kaufman.

The day arrived. I entered the cozy Lyceum Theatre and was presented to Kaufman by the stage manager. My idol merely peered over his glasses at me, nodded, and turned away. Undaunted, I took a seat at the side of the auditorium, hoping I would be unnoticed and could remain for the first reading of the play.

Valency was now with the great man. They were engaged in heated conversation. Kaufman turned away and Valency left the Lyceum on the run.

It struck me as strange that the adaptor did not remain for the rehearsal. Later I was told that he and Kaufman had been debating the meaning of the play. The director had seen it simply as a triangular love story, a point of view that so appalled Valency he abandoned ship.

Kaufman called the stage manager aside and whispered in his ear as he pointed to me. I got the message and left, deprived of the privilege of watching Kaufman at work.

From then on I returned to rehearsals only during breaks. Each time I greeted the director cheerily; he would only nod, and turn away. Our relationship, if not warm, was consistent.

The Enchanted opened in January and closed in February. It had been misdirected. Miss MacGrath was miscast. And Mr. Jones's setting was inappropriate. In the theatre, even the mighty have more misses than hits.

I was to work on three more Kaufman productions: *Guys and Dolls, Silk Stockings,* and *Romanoff and Juliet,* the last play to be directed by him. Each time we encountered each other, he nodded *twice* before turning away. He was getting to know me better, when time ran out.

Shakespeare Is Something That Closes Saturday Night

It took the courage of a Spartacus for producers Robert L. Joseph and Alexander H. Cohen to put together a commercial Broadway production of Shakespeare's *King Lear.* They engaged John Houseman to direct it and Marc Blitzstein to compose the original music and songs. They further distinguished it by signing a formidable cast. Louis Calhern played the title role, abetted by Jo Van Fleet, Nina Foch, and Edith Atwater as the king's daughters, Martin Gabel as Kent, Arnold Moss as Gloucester, Joseph Wiseman as Edmund, Nehemiah Persoff as Cornwall, and Norman Lloyd as the King's Fool.

One morning I picked up Calhern at his hotel to escort him to an interview. As we entered a taxicab, the driver turned around and said, "Hey, ain't you Louis Calhern, the actor? Whatcha doin' now?"

"I'm rehearsing *King Lear,*" replied Calhern, shooting

an accusing glance at me, since I was being paid to let the world know what he was doing.

"Is that right?" said the cabbie. "I once saw Thomashefsky do it down on Second Avenue. Ya think it'll go in English?"

As a matter of fact it didn't, despite the exceptional performances, the immaculate staging, and some pretty good reviews. Joseph always felt that Cohen had been too hasty in insisting that the closing notice be posted. A couple hundred prospective customers had to be turned away from the final performance, which was sold out. Cohen defended his action. "Anything can sell out on Saturday night," he said. "It's the following Monday night I'm worried about."

Theatregoers seem to like their Shakespeare performed in repertory in suburban sylvan settings. Houseman must have sensed that, for shortly afterward, he helped initiate the American Shakespeare Festival in Stratford, Connecticut, which Walter Kerr was later to refer to as "a cultural Howard Johnson's."

How Lucky Can an Actor Get?

Twilight Walk was an inconsequential play, one of those mid-September disasters that start off each theatre season as if it were the last. It was about a sex murderer who stalked Central Park. I rather imagine that Central Park was a safe place in which to stroll in the early evening hours, until this play was produced.

As *Variety* would put it, "*Twilight Walk* shuttered after eight perfs." The only thing I recall was the performance of a young unknown named Walter Matthau in the role of a detective. He was most convincing because he had been brought up on the Lower East Side, and a number of his boyhood buddies had become detectives. It was one of those neighborhoods that produced guys who either joined the police force or went to the electric chair. Matthau somehow had slipped between these two alternatives and become an actor.

Twilight Walk was the first of an extraordinary streak of failures for Matthau. Later that season he was to play an art critic in George S. Kaufman's *Fancy Meeting You Again* (eight performances), and a devious executive in *One Bright Day* (twenty-nine performances).

The following season he played an airline pilot in *In Any Language* (forty-five performances), a magazine writer in *The Grey-Eyed People* (five performances), and a middle-aged salesman in *A Certain Joy* (mercifully closed in Philadelphia, before ever reaching New York).

Six turkeys in two seasons must be worthy of mention in *The Guinness Book of World Records*. Now that he's a major film star, Matthau hasn't appeared in six flop movies among the many he's made. His name means money in the box office, but back in those early days on Broadway, he was box office poison.

Broadway's Grand Ole Opry

My Darlin' Aida was a *kamikaze* production. Basing a Broadway musical on Verdi's opera *Aïda*, switching its locale from Memphis, Egypt, to Memphis, Tennessee, and setting it in the American Civil War was about as sensible as mixing nitroglycerine in a blender. Yet enough curiosity-seekers and lovers of the Verdi score ventured into the Winter Garden, one of the few Broadway theatres actually on Broadway, to keep it open for eleven weeks following a critical bombardment comparable to the shelling of Fort Sumter.

Aïda is a staple in any opera repertoire, a surefire sellout when performed. To bring it to Broadway, though, and expect to become rich from it, requires the same optimism that permitted the Trojans to sleep peacefully through the night, convinced that the huge horse at the town gates was merely overweight.

Because its music made inordinate demands on its singers, *My Darlin' Aida* required alternates for many of its leading roles. Eight shows a week could strip even the sturdiest vocal cords. For example, opera stars Elaine Malbin and Dorothy Sarnoff sang only evening performances, substitutes singing the matinees. Miss Malbin was the beautiful and dignified Aida, slave girl of the Old South. Miss Sarnoff was Jessica Farrow, daughter of the plantation owner, General Farrow (Pharaoh, get it?). Two young tenors, Howard Jarratt and William Olvis, alternated in the role of Confederate Lieutenant Raymond Demarest (by any other name, still our old friend, Radames).

It was undecided who would play Demarest at the opening. Jarratt won by a toss of the coin. That evening, during his first big number (on Broadway they're called numbers; in grand opera, arias), sung to the tune of "Celeste Aïda," he cracked on a high note. Like Humpty-Dumpty, *My Darlin' Aida* never was able to put itself together again.

I do not mean to imply that poor Mr. Jarratt was solely responsible for the failure of the show; countless others before him have had their problems with that same high note. All I know is that I never did hear what became of him, once the show closed. On the other hand, Mr. Olvis, who watched the opening night performance from the back of the house, went on to sing at the Metropolitan Opera.

Not Even Houdini . . .

Carnival in Flanders was a musical adaptation of the exceptional French film, *La Kermesse Héroïque,* already high on the list of all-time screen classics. Preston Sturges was the adaptor and director of the musical, Johnny Burke wrote the lyrics, and Jimmy Van Heusen the music. Dolores Gray portrayed the wife of the mayor of a besieged sixteenth-century Flemish village, who cozies up to the invading Spanish duke, played by John Raitt, in order to dissuade him from burning and sacking the town.

To prepare for summer bookings in San Francisco and Los Angeles, the show first played in June to audiences in

Philadelphia. An immediate dud, it received little brotherly love from the local burghers. In the first two weeks of a three-week engagement, the cast outnumbered the audience. The nervous West Coast promoter tried frantically to escape his fate, and was making some legal headway.

At the beginning of the third week, Karl Bernstein called the company manager in Philadelphia to check the show's progress. Much to his amazement, he was told that it had closed the previous Saturday, and that the entire company had left town—bag, baggage, scenery, costumes, and imitation Flemish paintings. Hour by hour the mystery deepened. Nobody would come forth and explain what had happened to an entire $250,000 musical. Nor could we reach any member of the cast or company. "I've had many shows close on me in my time," said Karl quizzically, "but this is the first time I've ever had one disappear."

By Wednesday we were on the verge of giving the papers the most intriguing vanishing-act story since Judge Crater. Then, during a lunch-hour stroll, we saw the familiar face of one of the show's chorus dancers. We dashed across the street, grabbed him by the lapels, and demanded an explanation. "We're rehearsing up the block at the Century Theatre," he said. "Been there since Monday. The producers are waiting to find out about California. If we don't go, we'll probably fold."

We headed for the Century Theatre, where we found the shaken producer and the company manager. They claimed they had forgotten to advise us in the excitement of the sudden move from Philadelphia. The overpowering loneliness caused by empty houses had impelled them to depart that city.

The legal entanglements having been cleared up, *Carnival in Flanders* headed for California the following week as originally scheduled. For two months, panic reigned as repairs were made. To an objective viewer, the improvements were slight. The show opened in New York the Tuesday following Labor Day and closed that Saturday.

In a way, I have always regretted that *Carnival in Fland-*

ers did not disappear entirely that June. It would have made one helluva story.

'Twas a Season to Be Merry

The 1954-55 season was virtually devoid of professional tragedy for me. I worked on three musicals, all of which thrived. The first, a British import, *The Boy Friend*, introduced Julie Andrews to American audiences.

The Boy Friend was a musical pastiche of the 1920s. I am convinced that it is responsible for triggering the wave of nostalgia that reached tidal proportions in the 1970s. A deliberately puerile book and a charming score, both by Sandy Wilson, delighted audiences for fourteen months.

Silk Stockings was a musical adaptation of the Greta Garbo film *Ninotchka*, in which the Swedish star displayed her gift for comedy. The Broadway production starred the German actress Hildegarde Neff and screen actor Don Ameche, the butt of every bad telephone joke since he portrayed Alexander Graham Bell on the screen.

George S. Kaufman, with whom I now had a nodding acquaintance, and his wife, Leueen MacGrath, wrote the book of *Silk Stockings*, with Abe Burrows coming in to help when the show encountered Kaufman's trouble box in Philadelphia. An ailing libretto required a doctor, and Burrows had recently superseded Kaufman as Broadway's leading play-fixer.

Cole Porter wrote the music and lyrics, which, the critics agreed, were not up to his usual high standard. "They've written this about me ever since my second show," Porter said.

At the New York premiere of *Silk Stockings*, Burrows was asked how one could differentiate between what Kaufman and MacGrath wrote, and what he contributed. "When you laugh," he replied, preferring to leave the issue in doubt.

In the theatre, as in real life, you win some, you lose some. We all won with *Silk Stockings*, a show that could well have gone the other way. Porter was so exhausted from the extended tryout period that when asked to write a new song for a party scene in a Moscow apartment, he produced "The Red Blues," in which the only lyric was "I've Got the Red Blues," repeated over and over again.

My final show of the season was *3 for Tonight*, described in its program as a "Diversion in Song and Dance." Its title was perhaps a bit misleading, since the cast consisted of four, Marge and Gower Champion, Harry Belafonte, and Hiram Sherman.

One afternoon I escorted Belafonte to a studio, where he was to be photographed for the cover of the Sunday newspaper supplement *Parade*. The photographer objected to Belafonte's nondescript shirt, and I rushed to a men's store to buy him a vivid maroon job, cut down to his navel. I am not certain if it was the first such garment ever worn by the gifted performer, but low-cut shirts have been his trademark for as long as anyone can remember. Later, I bought one for myself, but somehow I never managed to look as good in it as Belafonte did.

Simon Doesn't Say

Catch a Star is never mentioned in any biographies of Neil Simon. Why he chooses to omit it puzzles me, since he can count his failures on one finger.

Catch a Star was a revue, a theatre form that has seen its day, but still flourishes on television. It lingered at the Plymouth Theatre for twenty-three poorly attended performances. Its program clearly stated, "Sketches by Danny and Neil Simon." Danny is Neil's brother.

Catch a Star wasn't unremittingly atrocious. Its humorous sketches indicated promise of better things to come for its writers. And no show featuring the late David Burns could be all bad. Witty, friendly, with a solid streak of hilarious vulgarity, Burns was an asset to any production. I cannot recall his ever giving a poor performance, and he was a master of the ad lib both on and off stage. In the relatively small world of show business, everybody was his friend.

On Wednesday afternoons before the matinee performance of *Catch a Star*, Burns would hold court on the sidewalk in front of the Plymouth's stage door, pontificating on all the problems of the world. One day he said to me, "I am beginning to doubt the value of oral communication, son. People talk to each other, but they don't grasp what the other person is saying. They only understand what they want to understand. In other words, it's not what you say, it's how you say it."

I challenged his theory, and he said, "Let me give you a practical example. Just wait a few minutes. Is it worth a five-dollar wager to you?"

I agreed to the bet, and before long, Burns spotted one of the show's chorus dancers walking down the block towards us, accompanied by an older woman. When she reached us, she said to Burns, "I want you to meet my mother, Mrs. Schlogheimer. She's seeing the matinee today."

"Ah, Mrs. Schlogheimer," he said cheerfully, "I'm delighted to make your acquaintance. I must tell you that your lovely daughter is the finest practitioner of fellatio in the entire company. We all adore her. You should be proud of her."

"Why thank you, Mr. Burns," the beaming mother said.

After she had entered the lobby, he turned to me, palm outstretched, and said, "What did I tell you? Give me the five, son."

The Best House Isn't Good Enough

Before the start of the 1956-57 season I had quit my job with Karl Bernstein and for the first time was on my own. Or so it seemed. Actually, all I had done was exchange a single boss for several. Call them clients, if you wish. But at last I was a full-fledged senior press agent, entitled to a ridiculously overblown title in the program—General Press Representative.

The "General" is intended to differentiate between the senior publicist and the associates who work under his supervision. Very likely the term came into use when a West Point dropout decided to seek his fortune in theatrical publicity.

The first play to bear the credit "General Press Representative . . . Harvey Sabinson" was *The Best House in Naples* by F. Hugh Herbert. A few years before, Herbert had written *The Moon Is Blue*, considered the *Deep Throat* of its time. By current standards, it would be a fitting nursery-school exercise.

The Best House in Naples was taken from an Italian play by Eduardo de Filippo, one of Italy's foremost commercial dramatists. It starred the Mexican actress Katy Jurado as a "kept" woman.

The gutsy producer, Nick Mayo, was a former stage manager of *South Pacific*, who decided to give me the job because "you'll break your ass on the first show of your own."

There was hardly time to make a dent in my posterior; the show opened Friday and closed Saturday.

Actually, an omen of disaster occurred at the first tryout performance at the Shubert-owned Walnut Street Theatre in Philadelphia. Before the curtain rose, Lawrence Shubert Lawrence, director of the theatrical family's Philadelphia operation, threw up on the sidewalk in front of the theatre. That was the high point of the evening.

Years later my wife and I went to see Sophia Loren and Marcello Mastroianni in a highly touted Vittorio de Sica film. It wasn't three minutes into the picture when I turned to her and whispered, "I've seen this before. She's an ex-whore who's been living with this rich guy for years. He won't marry her because of her past, so she pretends to be dying. As a last request, she asks him to marry her and make her an honest woman. In a deathbed ceremony the parish priest marries them, after which she hops out from under the blankets and says, 'I gotcha, you son of a bitch.' "

"Now you've gone and ruined it for me," she said, "But it sounds like *The Best House in Naples,* one of your biggest turkeys."

Indeed, the plots were the same. But the film was superb. It was called *Marriage, Italian Style.*

What's the Matter with the Critics?

David Merrick presented six shows during the 1958-59 season: *The World of Suzie Wong, Epitaph for George Dillon, Maria Golovin, La Plume de Ma Tante, Destry Rides Again,* and *Gypsy.* Of these, *Epitaph for George Dillon* is my favorite. I consider it the best of John Osborne's works.

George Dillon told the harrowing story of an egotistical writer who settles for being a hack, retreating into a self-imposed emotional dependency on a second-rate working-class family.

In the two previous seasons, Merrick had produced Osborne's *Look Back in Anger* and *The Entertainer.* We had great hopes for *George Dillon.*

The pre-Broadway tryout began at the Warner Theatre in Atlantic City, where a group of local promoters envisaged the rebirth of their city as a theatre capital. Atlantic City had been a "must" tour stop until the 1930s; then it quietly vanished from the route sheets.

The Warner was a large movie house, one of those tasteless Moorish imitations, erected during the twenties to accommodate a plethora of deMillian spectacles. Like the boardwalk and its bordering shops and hotels, the theatre was perilously close to total shabbiness. A sizeable audience for a play would be lost in the Warner's more than 3,000 seats. Certainly *George Dillon* was lost.

Before the curtain rose, I took a seat next to the playwright. He looked up at the theatre's ornate ceiling, complete with twinkling stars and drifting clouds. "I think it's going to rain," he said. "I'm getting out of here before it starts." He wisely left for a stroll on the boardwalk.

Although the weather indoors was never more than

partly cloudy, the play seemed murky in the mammoth auditorium.

After an equally dismaying fortnight at the crumbling old Ford's Theatre in Baltimore, we were relieved to arrive at the tiny John Golden Theatre on Manhattan's West Forty-fifth Street. The theatre and the play seemed to fit each other perfectly. The opening-night performance was a revelation as Eileen Herlie, Robert Stephens, and the rest of the cast worked together beautifully. We were convinced we had a hit.

The glow of success was brief. As I picked up the reviews one by one, I was shocked by the almost universal lack of critical enthusiasm. The reviewers had blown it. Like umpires, they occasionally call one wrong.

I am no great admirer of opening-night parties, but had committed myself to appear at the one being given for *George Dillon* to deliver the notices. Bearing such downbeat news, I knew that my arrival would turn the affair into a wake. As I entered the East Side apartment where the party was in full swing, I was greeted by Helen Hayes, an Osborne fan, who demanded a full report. When I told her, she accused me of making up some sick joke. Then she apologized, realizing how painful this mission was for me. As word spread, the party began to break up amid threats of physical mayhem against the critics.

Despite a groundswell of public support for the play, there was no appeal from the critical verdict. It was impossible to raise an audience. Merrick decided to close, but Marlene Dietrich parked herself in his office, demanding that he keep it alive. We managed to struggle through three weeks, then folded. Subsequent reincarnations of the play, both on and off Broadway, have enjoyed somewhat greater success, but the memory of that closing is still bitter.

In the same week that *George Dillon* opened, the following evening, in fact, Merrick presented Gian Carlo Menotti's opera *Maria Golovin,* about a blind birdcage maker. Because it was being offered on an eight-performance-a-week schedule at a Broadway theatre, Merrick and Menotti opted for the drama critics rather than the music reviewers. It made no difference. *Maria Golovin* was a bomb. Menotti never forgave Merrick for closing it within a week.

Two flops in one week can be hazardous to one's health. At the time, Merrick confided to me, "Now you know why I like a lot of action. By producing several plays I like during the same season, I'm bound to have a few hits. I don't think I could stand producing a single play a year like most producers. What's there to look forward to?"

Of the six he produced during that season, four were smash hits. *The World of Suzie Wong,* a tawdry piece about a Hong Kong hooker with a heart of jade, ran for fourteen months. But Merrick never seemed particularly proud of it. Sometimes the good die young and the sinners live to a ripe old age.

The Great Strike of 1960

"Boy, are you lucky," said the voice on the other end of the line. "You'll get all the space without even working for it."

It was Seymour Goodman, fellow publicist, colleague, rival, and rumormonger. "Sy, tell me what it is that makes me so lucky." I said. "I'm almost afraid to know."

"The way I hear it, your show is gonna be the first one struck," he said. "Equity is meeting tonight before show time, and while they won't call an official strike, the cast of just one play will not report to work. Equity hopes this will frighten the League enough to come across."

"So how does this make me lucky?" I asked again.

"The only show that's supposed to be affected is *The Tenth Man.* That's your show, isn't it? You'll get world-wide publicity." It was the first time that I had ever heard possible loss of income equated with good fortune.

Equity, the union of all professional stage actors, and the League of New York Theatres and Producers, the organization representing Broadway producers and theatre owners, had been engaged in collective bargaining for weeks. The issues were familiar—wages, working conditions, fringe benefits. Progress was slow, and the talks were becoming ugly as overly dramatic characters on each side of the table tossed demeaning insults at the opposition.

"We've got the highest unemployment figures in the nation," said the actors.

"That's because you have so many lousy actors who are unemployable," countered the producers.

"Production costs are so high because producers steal."

"If it weren't for producers, who would hire actors?"

The May 31 deadline had passed, casting a pall on the theatre district. Small groups huddled on the sidewalks, whispering their fears to each other. Emotion had replaced reason.

The 1959-60 season had started out like a house afire for me, with an all-star production of Shaw's *Heartbreak House*, which was followed by *Take Me Along*, a musical version of O'Neill's *Ah, Wilderness*, starring Jackie Gleason and Robert Morse. (The run of *Take Me Along* was spiced by a feud between the producer, David Merrick, and The Great One. When Gleason missed a few performances with what he claimed was an upset stomach, Merrick remarked, "Gleason with an upset stomach is like a giraffe with a sore throat.")

Then *The Tenth Man* opened to smash notices. It was an excellent piece by Paddy Chayefsky, dealing with dybbuks, possession, and exorcism, set in a grubby synagogue in the Williamsburg section of Brooklyn. The director was Sir Tyrone Guthrie, pride of the British theatre, who did his research by attending services in various Brooklyn synagogues. A tall, gaunt man, given to wearing sneakers on all occasions, he narrowly missed being bar mitzvahed on one of them when an eager rabbi offered to do it on the spot since he already had a *minyan* (the required quorum of men).

My winning streak came to a halt as I encountered five flops in a row, but things brightened a bit in May when a tiny musical called *The Fantasticks* opened in Greenwich Village. It was as shaky as a newborn chick at first, hanging on by a thread as the contract talks between Equity and the League heated up. The possibility of an actual strike, however, seemed remote to me, and my staff and I immersed ourselves in promoting *The Fantasticks* so that it could enjoy a bit of a run. (As of this writing, it is in its eighteenth year, and should continue far beyond the time when earthmen begin to use Mars as a garbage dump.)

On the afternoon of June 1, Arthur Cantor, coproducer of *The Tenth Man*, called me. "Better be at the theatre tonight," he said. "I hear our cast isn't showing up, and the press should be all over the place."

"Are they striking every show?" I asked.

"No," he replied, "my spies tell me that if no agreement is reached by early evening, Equity will hold an emergency membership meeting. As I understand it, they'll select one show for a walkout. I bet they pick *The Tenth Man*."

While it seemed unlikely that the battle noises being heard in Broadway would be of interest in the farmlands of Iowa, a massive showing of the media turned up that night in Shubert Alley, ready to tell the story to a less than anxiously waiting nation. TV crews, photographers, and reporters were milling about when I arrived at 7:45. (It should be noted that in those "civilized" days, theatre curtains rose at 8:30 or 8:40.)

At eight, the traditional "half-hour" time when all actors are required to be in the theatre preparing for the performance, the casts of all the shows on Forty-fourth and Forty-fifth Streets began reporting for work as usual, with the exception of the cast of *The Tenth Man*. "We're the Chosen People," remarked our general manager, Joe Harris.

Cantor and his coproducer, Saint-Subber, a shy theatre veteran with a long string of successes, decided to admit the audience in the faint hope that this was a scare tactic and that the company would appear by 8:30. The actors never arrived, and at the last minute, Cantor came to me and said, "I have to apologize to the audience. Give me something light and funny to say."

"That's easy," I said. "As the curtain rises on the synagogue set, revealing just you and Saint, repeat the opening lines of the Passover ceremony, 'Why then is this night different from all other nights?' Then go on to explain that the goddamn actors didn't show up, and that you will be happy to return everyone's money. But don't let it go at that Warn them that roughly 900 people will be lining up for refunds, and therefore it will take hours. So if they don't care to wait, they can mail in their tickets for exchange for a future performance."

Cantor looked dour. "That's shocking," he said, "and not very funny."

Undaunted, I came up with another suggestion. "When the curtain goes up and only you two characters are onstage, point out that he's a Saint, you're a Cantor, and this is a synagogue, but it's not enough to do a show. That should get a big laugh."

"Never mind," he said, "I'll think of something myself."

Cantor and Saint-Subber entered the stage door, and I escorted a platoon of press to the back of the house. The curtain rose to reveal two pale, nervous men in the hot glare of the stage lights. By now the audience was restless. "Ladies and gentlemen," Cantor began, "tonight's performance has been cancelled because our cast is on strike. You may obtain refunds at the box office or mail in your tickets for exchange. I'm sorry."

I thought to myself, now *that's* funny, as a disgruntled group of people filed out of the Booth.

The next night all the other Broadway shows closed

down in what was to be Broadway's first lengthy blackout since 1919. It lasted ten days and weakened some shaky shows so badly that they could never reopen. It cost producers and all other working theatre personnel ten days of income. But it proved one thing: without Broadway, New York is really Cleveland.

On the Beach

Sitting on a beach in the summer of 1960—Jones I think it was—I counted my future blessings. I was under contract to represent productions with some of the biggest names in show business. I turned to my wife and said, "None of this middle-class baloney for us anymore. Like no other season before, this one'll really put me in the bigtime.

"Listen to this lineup: *Kukla, Fran and Ollie,* with Burr Tillstrom and the Kuklapolitans; *An Evening with Mike Nichols and Elaine May;* Jack Lemmon, didja hear that, Jack Lemmon in *Face of a Hero;* Tennessee Williams's first comedy, *Period of Adjustment;* Julie Harris in *Little Moon of Alban;* Lucille Ball in *Wildcat;* Walter Matthau and Françoise Rosay in *Once There Was a Russian;* Jason Robards, Hume Cronyn, George Grizzard, and Martin Gabel in *Big Fish, Little Fish;* Zero Mostel, Eli Wallach, and Anne Jackson in *Rhinoceros.*

"Take a good look around you. No more Jones Beach for us—noisy transistor radios, crowded parking lots, sticky-fingered children. By spring we'll be able to buy a beach house in East Hampton, and a Mercedes to take us there."

"Don't count your turkeys before they're hatched," my very own Cassandra reminded me.

By the time autumn rolled around, my dreams began to fall like leaves. Nobody wanted to pay to see Tillstrom and his Kuklapolitans; they'd been given away free on TV for too long. The show was yanked after twenty-seven performances.

Nichols and May could have made it for an extended run, but they got bored with the act, maybe with each other, and quit after nine months. Elaine never forgave me after a magazine described her apartment as "a giant ashtray."

The very thought of Jack Lemmon playing a corrupt prosecutor repelled what otherwise might have been a huge audience. The screen's number one box-office star had miscalculated. He should have come to Broadway in a comedy, not a heavy drama. In less than two months, he was back on the West Coast.

I sensed something was wrong when Elia Kazan dropped out as director of his good friend Tennessee Williams's *Period of Adjustment* a few weeks before rehearsals were to begin. He was replaced by the talented George Roy Hill, who could not bring it off, saving his best shots for subsequent motion pictures like *Butch Cassidy and the Sundance Kid* and *The Sting*.

In *Period of Adjustment,* Williams wrote a good deal of banter about a matched set of bright blue luggage that belonged to one of the characters. The producer presented me with this luggage after the play's timely close. Those bags have been all over Europe, South America, and the United States with me, serving as a reminder that although he is our foremost dramatist, Williams is no Neil Simon when it comes to comedy.

The short-lived production of *Little Moon of Alban* was a stage version of a highly acclaimed original TV play about the "troubles in Ireland." Borrowing from television was a novel switch for the theatre. To make people feel at home, I suggested to the producer that we place fruit-laden refrigerators in the lobby. She considered it for a while, but then wisely decided to fold.

Playing eight performances a week in *Wildcat* exhausted Lucille Ball so that she was compelled to quit after less than six months on Broadway and to return to the relatively leisurely pace of a half-hour weekly TV show.

Once There Was a Russian lived up to its title. It was seen but *once* on Broadway. With a Russian accent like a dialect comedian's, Walter Matthau played Count Potemkin, advisor to Catherine the Great, portrayed by the legendary French star Mme. Rosay, with authentic Parisian accent. It was an unintelligible combination.

Big Fish, Little Fish had outstanding performances, a fair script by Hugh Wheeler, and John Gielgud as director. With a subplot of homosexuality, it lacked only public acceptance.

Rhinoceros, Eugene Ionesco's comic attack on conformity, was produced by Leo Kerz, an intense man who doubled as scene designer. In addition to Mostel and the Wallachs, the cast also included Jean Stapleton, later to become television's favorite dingbat, Mrs. Archie Bunker.

This production by Ionesco, an exponent of the Theatre of the Absurd, began to take on overtones of absurdity from the start. The Franco-Rumanian playwright attended the first meeting of the cast. For twenty minutes he spoke on the meaning of his play—in French, and without benefit of an interpreter. Then the cast was given time for questions. Only Mostel made any sense when he yelled out, "Would you repeat that, please?"

Kerz announced that no matter how good the notices, he would not take a quote ad to promote the play, but instead would make available to interested parties unedited reprints of the notices. While this was an audacious and forthright step, it dismayed the cast. Actors like to see all the good things written about them in one large advertisement. They immediately organized an anti-Kerz front. For them, communications had broken down in two areas —first with the playwright and now with the producer.

After only a single weekend of previews, in lieu of the usual two- or three-week tryout, the play opened to mainly favorable notices. Kerz began to distribute his reprints under the ponderous title "For the Benefit of Skeptics Who Doubt *Rhinoceros* Received What Probably Amounts to the Best Reviews of Any Play This Season." Up to that point I had not been aware of any skeptics.

The cast rebelled and called a meeting before a Wednesday matinee. Wallach asked me to attend to supply some information on advertising costs. "We're considering buying our own ad," he explained.

The meeting was held on the stage of the Longacre Theatre. Kerz got wind of it. Hiding behind a translucent curtain, he was a conspicuous eavesdropper. When he was pointed out, somebody roared, "What difference does it make? Let him stay and play Polonius."

"How much would it cost to run a half-page in the *Times*?" Wallach asked me.

"About four thousand bucks," I said.

"And a quarter of a page?"

"Two thousand."

He whistled and said, "That's a lot of money."

I left before a decision was reached, but thereafter Kerz considered me a traitor to his cause. Although the cast never bought the ad, he harassed me for weeks. When I submitted an expense item for a luncheon interview for Wallach, he refused to pay it, saying, "Wallach should pay for his own interview."

Such pettiness made my position untenable, and for the first time in my life, I resigned from a show. Like castor oil, Kerz was a little hard for me to take.

Rhinoceros ran on Broadway for 241 performances. By early the following summer, all those promising shows had disappeared from my life, and I was back on the beach. Coney Island this time.

The Hemingway Pictures

"How can I get some up-to-date pictures of Hemingway, Hotch?" I asked.

"Call Ernest in Idaho and tell him what you need," he said. "If he's not in, Mary'll take care of it. I'll give you the number."

A. E. Hotchner, magazine editor, free-lance writer, dramatist, first met Ernest Hemingway in 1948 when he went to Cuba to ask him to do an article for *Cosmopolitan*. In later years, they became close friends, and Hotchner dramatized many of Hemingway's works for television. Now he was working on a project for the theatre, a piece to be called *A Short Happy Life*, based on Hemingway short stories and characters. It was scheduled to open in Seattle in early September, tour down the West Coast, and then come to New York.

The stage never seemed to do justice to Hemingway. The movies succeeded from time to time, but all he had to show for his work in the theatre was one original play in 1940, *The Fifth Column*, about the Spanish loyalists, and a 1930 adaptation of *A Farewell to Arms*.

"Don't call him Papa," warned Hotchner. "His best friends call him Ernest. Those who think they're his friends call him Papa."

"If it's all the same to you," I said, "I'll just call him Mr. Hemingway."

Hemingway himself took my call. His tone was friendly, although I had been told that he was not fond of telephone conversations. He said, "I think I have what you want. Recently had some pictures taken by Karsh. Damn good shots. Miss Mary'll put them in the mail today."

"One more thing, Mr. Hemingway," I said. "I got a call from a lady in Seattle, where we open. She wants you to stay on her yacht on Lake Washington when you come out there in September."

"Find out more about it," he said, "and call me in August."

A large brown envelope arrived on July 1 just before I was to leave with my family for a week's fishing trip to Seneca Lake in upstate New York. It contained six copies of a magnificent portrait of Hemingway, taken by the gifted Yousuf Karsh. It was the most impressive photograph I had ever seen. He wore an Aran sweater whose wide turtleneck framed his wiry gray beard. His eyes were filled with loneliness and gentleness at the same time.

I placed the photographs in a folder and secured them in a file cabinet. The next day, as we headed north on the thruway, a radio report blared the news of the death of Ernest Hemingway, by his own hand, at age sixty-two. I pulled over to the side of the road and reflected for a few minutes about a man I had never met except through his writings, a man who wanted no more of his life.

As a theatre piece, *A Short Happy Life* was insufficient. With a cast that included Rod Steiger and Keir Dullea, it opened on schedule in Seattle, and closed in Los Angeles in October. It never got to New York. The enthusiasm all of us had for the project back in the spring months had vanished with the death of Hemingway.

Five of the six Karsh portraits were distributed to the press in Los Angeles and Seattle. The sixth I kept for myself. Some years later I had the good fortune to meet and befriend Yousuf Karsh, the genius who had taken the photograph. He presented me with a copy of his book, *Faces of Our Time*, which contained the Hemingway portrait. Karsh wrote about his subject with great affection: "I found a man of peculiar gentleness, the shyest man I ever photographed. On developing my negatives I liked best the portrait printed here. It is, I think, a true portrait, the face of a giant cruelly battered by life."

9

The Bold and the Blue

Max Rosegarden, the producer, was on the phone, "Get your ass over here on the double. The billing is all screwed up."

His panic was infectious. "That can't be," I said. "Give me five minutes and I'll be there."

I grabbed my coat and ran for the elevator, with my secretary hard on my heels. "When will you be back?" she wanted to know.

"Probably never. Call my wife and tell her I want my body cremated. Give all my files to the public library, and tell the bookkeeper to give you two weeks' severance pay."

As the elevator door closed, I could hear her say, "I'll give your wife that message. Should she expect you for dinner?"

My office was on the West Side, Max's on the East Side. To save time, I hailed a taxi and barked at the driver, "Six forty-two Lexington Avenue and step on it." Ten minutes later we were still in front of my building. I slipped the driver a buck, got out, and ran across town.

I was breathless and sweaty when I reached Max's, where I found him in the midst of a severe anxiety attack. "Sit down," he said, pointing to an overstuffed vinyl-covered chair facing his desk. "I'll try to compose myself and discuss this disaster with you calmly and quietly. Did you read the billing clause in Walter Pollack's contract? Did you? Did you?"

"Sure I did," I replied. "I read everybody's billing clause. How else could I lay out all the ads and posters?"

"Then how come on the posters, Pollack's name is in green and the title of the play is in blue?" he asked.

"What's wrong with that?"

"What's wrong with that, you ask. If you have to ask, it proves you don't know what you're doing. Pollack's agent called me at eight o'clock this morning. Last night he went to have dinner at Sardi's. He saw a poster next door, in the ticket broker's window. After that he couldn't enjoy his dinner. He read me the billing clause in Walter's contract. It clearly says, 'Your credit shall appear last, on a separate line on which no other words or names shall appear. . . . ' "

"So?"

"Wait a minute! You didn't let me finish. ' . . . and shall be in the same boldness and prominence of type and at least fifty percent of the size of the largest letter of the billing used for the title of the play or the separate names of not more than two stars, or any credit, whichever is largest, but never less in size than the credit for the author whether or not the said author's name is above or below the title.'

"Did you hear that? 'The same boldness. The same *boldness.*' That damn agent and Walter Pollack claim that green is not the same boldness as blue. They're insisting that all the posters be destroyed, and that new ones be printed—with Walter's name in blue. They cost a thousand dollars. Where am I gonna get another thousand dollars? *You* should pay for them."

"Max, t-take it easy," I stammered. "It seems to me that green is as bold as blue. How important could this possibly be?"

"Not very, to *you*. To *them*, it's a catastrophe. We're not dealing with people. We're dealing with artists. It took me six months to convince Pollack to direct this play. He spent five weekends as my guest in Amagansett. He's the hottest director in the business today. Not the best, just the hottest. After he agreed, it took two months to negotiate his contract. We're still in rehearsal with this play. I need him more than he needs me. If he quits because his name is in green and not blue, the fate of this production is on your head."

"What if I can prove that green is as bold as blue?" I asked.

"If you can convince them of that, you'll save me a lot of *tsouris*," he said. "But I defy you to do it."

"Let me go back to my office and figure it out," I said. "You'll hear from me."

"All right. Work on it. Billing problems," he moaned. "They'll kill me someday."

Billing has always been of paramount importance to actors, playwrights, directors, and other creative artists. Apart from its influence on ego and prestige, it also has to do with future earnings and is, therefore, very much a business decision. Like money, it is a negotiable item. To most theatre professionals, it sometimes has a value greater than money.

Billing can become the *bête noir* of the publicist. Practically speaking, he should take courses in contract law to equip himself to interpret the legal curve balls tossed by attorneys and agents.

Karl Bernstein liked to tell of the time he saved the 1936 Cole Porter musical, *Red, Hot and Blue!* It starred Ethel Merman, Jimmy Durante, and Bob Hope. Either through a slip of the tongue, or a misplaced finger on the typewriter, both Miss Merman and Mr. Durante were guaranteed first star billing above the title.

There are no such things as ties in show business; the game is played to a sudden-death conclusion. Both parties and their agents, however, were immobile. Vinton Freedley, the producer, dumped this hot coal in Karl's lap.

Give Karl a pencil and a piece of paper and you can be sure he will design an ad. He enjoys drawing rough layouts. Ad agency art departments consider him a pain in the neck because they lack respect for a press agent's graphic talents. Undaunted, Karl went into seclusion with pencil and paper to seek a satisfactory compromise. After a few days, he emerged and proudly presented his solution to Mr. Freedley. He had drawn the following:

JIMMY MERMAN
ETHEL DURANTE
BOB HOPE
in
RED, HOT AND BLUE!

Both parties accepted Karl's resolution. Each was firmly convinced that first star billing was his or hers alone.

In 1951, Karl and I were handed a beaut. During a lull in their respective picture careers, and before they enjoyed some success in television, Ann Sothern and Robert Cummings agreed to co-star on Broadway in a comedy called *Faithfully Yours*. It was written by the Hungarian playwright, L. Bush-Fekete, and Mary Helen Fay, who, for all I know, was Mrs. L. Bush-Fekete. A description of the play's setting will tell you all you need to know about its plot: "The entire action takes place Today in the living room of the Hardings' penthouse in New York City." Miss Sothern's and Mr. Cumming's agents and lawyers grappled for days about which one was to be billed first. Finally a compromise was reached, without regard to the shattered nerves it would inflict upon innocent third parties, namely the press agents. Miss Sothern and Mr. Cummings agreed that they would alternate first star billing on a daily basis. (It has occurred to me that the odd-even day gas rationing plan instituted during the Great Gasoline Shortage of 1974 must, in some way, have been based on the Sothern-Cummings billing clauses.)

Karl and I were entrusted with the responsibility of seeing that each day's ad alternated the order of the stars' names, that a correct and different set of *Playbills* was distributed at the theatre at each performance, that the marquee of the Coronet (now the O'Neill) Theatre was switched daily, and that any news release we wrote on any given day had the proper billing order.

After a few weeks, we began to lose our minds. When I arrived at the office in the morning, Karl would be sitting there with a worried, puzzled look on his face. "Is today S-Day or C-Day?" he would ask.

Having determined which was which, we would nervously check the morning newspaper ads. (There were days when the papers could not keep up with this madness, prompting hostile phone calls from the actors' agents, who policed us carefully.) Then I would visit the Coronet Theatre to make sure that the house electrician was on his ladder changing the marquee. "This is a pain in the ass, you know," he would yell down to me.

I'd say, "To hell with you. At least you get paid overtime every time you go up there."

The odd-even day gas rationing ploy successfully eliminated long lines at service stations. Fortunately for us, the critics' reviews of *Faithfully Yours* eliminated long lines at the Coronet. The show closed in eight and a half weeks, just before the show's press agents might have been carried from the office, kicking and screaming.

I have no wish to get into an argument over who has the biggest name: Robert Shaw, Hume Cronyn, or Hume's wife, Jessica Tandy. All three are superb actors—the very best. If I am partial to Mr. Cronyn and Ms. Tandy, it is only because they are personal friends and two of the dearest people in the world. All three were signed to star in a 1964 production of *The Physicists*, by the Swiss playwright, Friedrich Duerrenmatt. Nobody wished to be difficult, but there seemed to be no easy answer as to which should receive first position in the billing. An alphabetical arrangement would naturally have suited the Cronyns, since they never have intra-family billing squabbles. He usually goes first.

Hume suggested that he and I sit down at lunch and quietly try to reach a satisfactory solution. After a forgettable meal, we came up with a proposal that Mr. Shaw found acceptable, as follows:

HUME
ROBERT   CRONYN   JESSICA
SHAW   TANDY

in
THE PHYSICISTS

Shaw was happy because he was first. Cronyn was happy because he was highest. Ms. Tandy was happy because her husband was happy.

Ten years later the Cronyns were to use a similar billing format when they co-starred with Anne Baxter in *Nöel Coward in Two Keys.*

I have read billing clauses that were impossible to comply with. That an actor is entitled to first billing in all press releases in no way guarantees a newspaper will carry it exactly that way—particularly if the drama editor loathes the actor. On occasion, I have noticed that a star's clause, guaranteeing him or her 100 percent of the title billing, will restrict any other actor in the show from receiving billing as large. Along comes the second star, who now has no alternative but to accept a smaller size, and agrees to 95 percent. Everybody is fairly happy—except the press agent. It is graphically possible to make one name 95 percent of the other in promotional material where the size of the letters is an inch or more. But what happens in the small daily newspaper alphabetical listings? Only a glib tongue and an appeal to rationality can soothe the aggrieved party who has been done out of the five percent advantage he had been holding.

There is an internationally famous director-choreographer whose billing clause always specifies that his name shall be "in a box." Surrounding it with ruled lines on all four sides is calculated to set his name off from all others in the same size. Those of us who have become entangled in the webs of billing are convinced that when he dies, his tombstone will bear his name—in a box.

Slowly I walk back, trying to come up with an idea that would save my ass and Max's money, or, to be more truthful, Max's backers' money. To refresh my memory, I asked my secretary for a copy of Pollack's billing rider. Carefully I began to read it:

> With respect to each company of the play in the United States, Canada, and elsewhere directed by you hereunder, you shall receive billing in all theatre programs, playbills, souvenir books, souvenir programs, marquees (except as hereinafter set forth below), display, window cards, three (or other dimension) sheets, posters, houseboards, billboards, and in all other paid advertising inclusive of the daily ABC (alphabetical listings) ads in all newspapers, or any type publicity and/or advertising issued by or under the control of the producer (including, but not in limitation of the foregoing, all ads and publicity wherever the name of the play is mentioned) and such credit shall be as follows:

Directed by WALTER POLLACK

I had read bicycle-assembling instructions that were clearer, and this was only the first paragraph. Already its legal mumbo-jumbo and redundancies had me baffled. Once before I had read this clause and no doubt had convinced myself that I understood its essence. Now, in my complete hysteria, its meaning eluded me. A meticulously devious legal mind was showing off here, and it was more than I, a math major who had mastered integral calculus and the functions of a complex variable, could handle. Heretofore, I had always considered theatre programs and playbills to be one and the same thing. "Souvenir books" was a synonym for souvenir programs. All this, however, did not clear up the matter of boldness.

Rather than trust my own poor judgment any further, I decided to consult my personal attorney in the hope that he would be able to decipher what Pollack's attorney had in mind. "I'm free today," he said, "and if you're buying, let's make it at 12:30 in the Oak Room of The Plaza."

By the time he arrived, at 1:00, I had already downed two vodka martinis. "Sorry I'm late, old buddy, but I got tied up in a hassle with the Theatre Guild," he said.

"Billing problems?" I inquired.

"How did you know?"

"Order yourself a drink and read this," I said, handing him Pollack's rider.

After a few minutes, he looked up and said, "The first paragraph is as plain as the ears on your head." (It should be noted that the ears on my head are partially obscured by a semi-mod hair-styling job that sets me back fifteen dollars a shot.) "All this lawyer is saying," he continued, "is that the director must receive billing everywhere."

"All right, Clarence Darrow," I said. "Let me read the next paragraph to you:

> If the theatre marquee is an electric or so-called lighted marquee, you shall not be entitled to receive any billing thereon, unless any names other than the theatre, title of the play, and the names of not more than two stars appear thereon.

"This is even clearer than the first clause," my lawyer friend remarked. "It means that the director does *not* have to receive billing everywhere. His name may be omitted from the marquee if all other conditions are fulfilled. Take my advice. Put his name on the marquee. He'll love you for it. Now, let's order."

He was playing with his escargots when I read paragraph three to him:

> The provisions above shall not apply to two-column newspaper or periodical teaser ads of three inches or forty-two lines in height or less, where such ads contain only the title of the play, the name of the theatre, the names of not more than two stars, the address and phone number of the theatre, and several quotes, or to Sunday ABC ads in any Sunday newspaper editions which carry also display ads for the play, which display ads include director's credit for you, unless the author receives credit in such Sunday ABC ads.

The legal eagle rose to the occasion. "This one gives you the opportunity to give him the finger if you feel like it. Just don't run any ads bigger than three inches. I wonder if the Chateaubriand is any good today?"

"Now here's the part that's giving me all the aggravation," I said, and read him the final paragraph, which Max had acupunctured into my brain.

"What do they mean by 'boldness'?" he asked. I suddenly realized that I had wasted a thirty-dollar lunch.

"I think they mean prominence, conspicuousness, maybe the same color, or another color as vivid," I replied. "Now let me ask you the big question. Is green as bold as blue?"

"Search me. I think you should consult an authority on art and color. Why don't you call Tom Hoving at the Metropolitan Museum? He'd make an excellent character or expert witness when this case reaches court."

Popping two Gelusils into my mouth in lieu of dessert, I said, "You've been a great help. Thanks a million."

"Any time," he said. "Let's do it again, real soon."

Later that day it occurred to me that his suggestion was not farfetched. I didn't know Tom Hoving, but I was acquainted with Lucille Steinritz, who ran a small gallery on East Fifty-seventh Street. I went to see her.

"I'm so glad you came to see our collages," she said as she greeted me.

"That's not exactly why I'm here. I must ask your opinion. Is green as bold as blue?"

"It depends on the shade," she replied.

"*Dark* green, and *dark* blue," I said.

"It's a matter of opinion. Some people might consider green bolder than blue. Others, blue bolder than green. If you mix yellow with blue, you get green, you know."

"That's interesting," I said, "but it doesn't solve the problem." I thanked her, and started down the stairs. "Aren't you going to look at the collages?" she yelled after me.

Was I enmeshed in a battle I could never hope to win? Don't fight it any more, I told myself. Maybe there was a way to make Pollack's name blue without spending another thousand dollars. I went down to lower Manhattan to see Harold Friedlander, my printer.

Over the clatter of the presses, I explained the situation. He came up with a possible solution. "Let me print strips in the right color with 'Clean-Stik' adhesive on the back and paste them over all the posters. It shouldn't cost more than fifty dollars, and it'll look fairly good. Maybe that'll satisfy everybody."

"Go to it, my friend," I told him. "It's now Tuesday. The play opens in New Haven on Saturday. Could they be ready in time? What I could do is take some of them with me to New Haven, and paste them on myself."

My mood improved considerably. There seemed no point in telling Max until the job was done. He would be leaving for New Haven with the company the following morning. I'd let him concentrate on getting the play on the stage and surprise him with the good news on Saturday evening just before the opening performance.

When I reached New Haven on Saturday morning, the manager of the Shubert Theatre gave me a list of thirty-five places that were displaying our posters. Not trusting the job to anyone else, I spent the better part of the day pasting on the new strips. My sticky journey took me to two hotels, three motor inns, twelve restaurants, four record shops, the Yale campus, eight luncheonettes, three department stores, and two boutiques. I got to know New Haven and its entrepreneurs as never before.

Worn out, but delighted with myself, I returned to the Shubert around 6:30. Max was pacing the lobby. Proudly, I told him, "You'll be happy to know that Walter Pollack's name is now in blue on every goddamn poster we had printed, and it cost practically nothing."

"I couldn't care less," he said, making an obscene gesture. "I just fired the son of a bitch."

10

Seven out of Seven

I arrived in Boston slightly unnerved and with little enthusiasm for the job at hand. The musical *Subways Are For Sleeping* had opened—to intense animosity—two nights before in Philadelphia. Like the New York City subway system it attempted to glorify, it was without apparent virtue, and in deep trouble. In less than four weeks, it would be inflicted upon the theatregoers of Boston.

Subways Are For Sleeping was "inspired," to use the word with supreme looseness, by a book of considerable charm and inconsiderable content by Edmund Love, a laconic man given to browsing through New York as if it were a secondhand bookshop. Having earned a bit of money from his writings, Love was now embarked on an extremely hazardous undertaking. He was eating his way through all the restaurants listed in the classified telephone books of New York City, one a day, from A to Z. This ambitious project, that could take at least a lifetime, or at the *very* least a life, intrigued me. When I asked him why, he merely replied, "Because they're there."

David Merrick realized he had acquired little more than a title when he bought the stage rights to Love's book. He commissioned Betty Comden and Adolph Green to flail it into an acceptable libretto, and Jule Styne to write the music. Michael Kidd was engaged to direct a cast that included Carol Lawrence, Sydney Chaplin (one of Charlie's boys), Phyllis Newman (Adolph Green's wife), and Orson Bean. The show was one of many Merrick entries during the 1961-62 season.

In blind obeisance to that threadbare theatrical code, "the show must go on," I was in Boston to alert its unsuspecting citizenry to the arrival of this expensive charade. Since Philadelphia is but 325 miles away, I had to move fast before the "word" beat me to it.

The Boston press usually plays it straight. They claim no prejudice because of a show's gloomy history prior to landing on the shores of Massachusetts Bay. Therefore I was greeted not as the advance man for a traveling leper colony, but as the emissary of a perfectly respectable enterprise. My stores of photographs and feature stories were accepted with grace and interest. All was going well until I reached the desk of Cyrus Durgin, urbane critic of the *Globe*.

Durgin and I exchanged the usual pleasantries as he sifted through my material, selecting what he considered appropriate for the drama pages of his paper. Shuffling my photographs, he looked up and said, "There is a conflict on the night your show opens. The Netherlands Chamber Orchestra is playing its only Boston concert that evening. After grappling with the problem, I have come to the conclusion that I will attend the concert. My assistant, Kevin Kelly, will cover *Subways Are For Sleeping*."

"Mr. Merrick won't like it," I said.

"That's tough," countered Durgin, biting down hard on his pipe stem, "I don't work for David Merrick. I'll cover the event I deem more important to the Boston cultural scene."

This convinced me that the bad news from Philadelphia had overtaken me in the homestretch.

"Then I take it you have no objection if I alert my master to this extraordinary state of affairs," I said. "He detests surprises—unless they come in the form of unexpected hit shows."

"Not at all," said Durgin. "Tell him anything you want. Also tell him that I consider Kevin a highly competent critic. Musicals try out in Boston year after year, but we don't often get a distinguished foreign ensemble like the Netherlands Chamber Orchestra."

The gauntlet was flung, leaving me no alternative but to pick it up and carry it back to Philadelphia where Merrick was regrouping his demoralized forces, urging them to dismiss from their minds all thoughts of defeat. "The show is a monumental disaster," he exhorted his troops. "Get it fixed before we open in Boston, or I'll close it here."

I reported my findings in the colony to the north. "How can Durgin send a second-string critic to review a half-million dollar musical?" Merrick lamented. "I consider it an affront to me and to the Broadway theatre. I won't have it. You can head right back to Boston and tell him that if he doesn't see fit to cover it himself, I will bar Kevin What's-His-Name."

Mounting my erratic steed, the New Haven Railroad, I returned to Boston to resume negotiations. They collapsed completely when Durgin, every part of him clenched, muttered, "The nerve of that man trying to tell me how to do my job. It's Kelly, and that's final."

Subways Are For Sleeping managed to survive the Philadelphia run. It arrived in Boston lightly buffed and begging for a fresh chance. On opening night Merrick set up a defensive perimeter in the lobby of the Colonial Theatre. An outpost was to be manned by a lone, unarmed vassal— me.

"When Kelly gets here," said Merrick, "tell him there is no ticket for him. If he wants to know why, tell him I consider him incompetent. If he becomes difficult, throw him out bodily. If you need me, I'll be there in the lobby."

At 7:30 Kelly arrived, apprehensive but not exactly shaking with fear. I repelled him at the outer breastworks. To his rear was a general assignment reporter for the *Globe* recording every word of our brief volley. When the reporter requested an interview with Merrick, I summoned my peerless leader, who valiantly stuck to his guns. "Mr. Durgin has insulted me and my production by sending an incompetent to review it," he said.

Not since Marshal Foch uttered his famous rallying cry, *"Ils ne passeront pas,"* has terrain been held with such fervor. Certain that he would never penetrate this wall of resistance, Kelly turned on his heels and retreated.

The skirmish won, Merrick and I entered the theatre. As the house lights dimmed and the overture began, I headed for the cozy confines of the manager's office. "Where are you going, son?" he asked. "Aren't you watching the show tonight?"

"I saw it in Philadelphia," I replied. "I'm eligible for leave."

As I opened the office door, Merrick was right behind me. Discretion dictated that he, too, should seek refuge lest the audience become hostile.

"When we open in New York, I'd honestly prefer to have the second-string critics there," I said to him. "This show could bring out the killer instinct in Taubman, Kerr, and that gang."

Merrick offered no response. Pulling a Manhattan telephone directory from an overhead shelf, he sat down at the manager's desk and began to read. Within moments a smile creased his face. It was apparent that he was deriving great pleasure from reading the phone book.

He looked up and said, "Do you recall when I used to ask you weekly when Brooks Atkinson was going to retire as critic of the *Times?*"

"Yes," I replied, "and when it finally happened, you seemed strangely overjoyed."

"I never told you at the time why I wanted to know," he said. "For a long time I've had this idea in the back of my mind. Now, with Atkinson out and Howard Taubman in, I'm convinced it can work."

"What can work? This show?"

"No, no, no. My idea." His voice dropped to a soft whisper as he divested himself of his great inner secret. "I think it is possible to find seven people with exactly the same names as the seven daily newspaper critics.

"Already I've found a Walter Kerr, several Robert Colemans, a Richard Watts, and loads of John Chapmans in the Manhattan book. I'm willing to bet that we can locate a Howard Taubman somewhere in the metropolitan area."

"Why was it so important for Atkinson to retire?" I asked.

"Because in all this world there is no other man with that name," he said. "I was hoping that his replacement would have a fairly common name . . . Now move your chair closer. I'm going to whisper the rest to you."

Rejecting my offer to sit in his lap, he resumed. "You mustn't breathe a word of this to anybody. Not to your wife, not to your partner, not to anyone on your staff. If it gets out, the idea is dead. I want you to contact seven people with the same names as the critics. Invite them to a preview performance in New York, as my guests. Take them out after the show to some expensive place like the Oak Room. Then get their written permission to quote them in an ad. I want to form my own critics' circle."

"It's absolutely brilliant, David," I said.

"Wait! I'm not finished. Do some research. Go through reviews of shows like *My Fair Lady, Oklahoma!, South Pacific.* Pick out the wildest praise from there and we'll attribute it to *Subways* from *our* critics.

"I've been dreaming about this for a long time. It wouldn't work with a good show, but with a dubious prospect like this, it just might come off. Now remember, not a word to anybody."

"Just one question, David," I said. "What if we get good notices in New York?"

"Don't talk nonsense," he replied.

The following morning I brought the Boston reviews of *Subways* to Merrick's suite at the Ritz-Carlton Hotel. Immaculate in his Savile Row pin-striped, hand-tailored suit, he said, "You don't have to tell me what fell apart today. I'm sure the reviews are dreadful."

"Most of the critics hated it," I said. "But I'm still in shock from reading the *Globe*. There's a rave in it and it's by Kevin Kelly."

"Impossible," said Merrick. "He didn't see it."

"Apparently he did. Last week in Philadelphia. After I warned Durgin that we'd bar the second-stringer, he sent Kelly to Philadelphia. Since we were sold out, he bought a standing-room ticket for last Saturday's matinee—and adored the show. He tells the whole story here in his review. There's also an accompanying item in which you're quoted as calling him incompetent."

Merrick smiled at this irony. "Doesn't his good review of this bomb prove him incompetent?"

With few tickets left for the Boston engagement because of a huge advance sale, my work there was done. Merrick suggested that I return to New York on the next plane to begin the quest for the "magnificent seven."

In 1961, before strikes and high operating costs whittled the number to three, Manhattan boasted seven daily newspapers. At the *Times*, Howard Taubman; Walter Kerr for the *Herald-Tribune;* John Chapman for the *Daily News;* Robert Coleman for the *Daily Mirror;* John McClain for the *Journal-American;* Norman Nadel for the *World-Telegram;* and Richard Watts for the *Post*.

Within a few hours I managed to locate my surrogate critics. Kerr, Watts, Chapman, and Coleman were listed in Manhattan, Taubman in the Bronx, McClain in Old Tappen, New Jersey, and Nadel in Union, New Jersey. A typical phone conversation follows:

"Hello, is this Walter Kerr?"

"Yes, who is this?"

"My name is Harvey Sabinson. I'm the press agent for David Merrick's Broadway production, *Subways Are For Sleeping*."

"I hate subways. I always try to take the bus."

"It's a Broadway show."

"Never heard of it. We don't go much to the theatre."

"It hasn't opened yet. That's probably why you haven't heard of it. It's being produced by David Merrick. You must have heard of him?"

"I think I once saw him being interviewed on television. Funny fellow with a black moustache?"

"Yes, that's him. Let me tell you why I'm calling, Mr. Kerr. Are you aware that there's a drama critic with the same name as yours?"

"I understand there is. Fellow works for the *Tribune*? I read the *Times*."

"Well, Mr. Merrick would like to invite you and Mrs. Kerr to see a preview performance of *Subways Are For Sleeping*. Is there a Mrs. Kerr?"

"Has been for eighteen years. But we don't go much to the theatre. Last show we saw was *Oklahoma!* Cost us twenty dollars including dinner."

"Well, this won't cost you a cent. Free down-front orchestra seats. Supper after the show at The Plaza. We'll even pay for taxis to get you to and from the theatre."

"Yeah? What's the catch?"

"There isn't any. All you have to do is come to see the show as our guests and then, if you like it, give us permission to use your name with a statement praising it."

"Oh, you mean like those ads in the papers?"

"Exactly."

"Sounds fishy to me. What's the catch?"

"It's just a little joke we want to play on the critics. We're inviting seven gentlemen with the same names as the seven daily newspaper critics. You won't be alone. And there's nothing for you to do except enjoy the show."

"What if we don't like it?"

"Then there's no obligation. Nobody will pressure you."

"Doesn't sound right to me."

"Believe me, there's nothing wrong with it, and you'll have a chance to see a big Broadway musical before it opens."

" . . . I guess we have nothing to lose—except an evening at home. When can we go?"

"Any night that's convenient for you week after next."

"How's Tuesday?"

"Okay. Just look for me in the lobby of the St. James Theatre on West Forty-fourth Street next to the ticket taker. I'll be wearing a blue blazer with gray slacks."

"Do we ask for our tickets at the box office?"

"No, don't go to the box office. I'll have your tickets with me. Just look for me."

"What if there's another guy in the lobby with a blue blazer and gray slacks?"

"I'm the one who'll be frowning. Just ask the ticket taker for me. You have my name?"

"No, I didn't catch it."

"It's Harvey Sabinson."

"Okay, Mr. Samuelson, we'll see you a week from Tuesday."

"Don't worry about a thing, Mr. Kerr. I'll send you a confirming letter with all the details. Oh, one more thing. Don't breathe a word of this to anybody. Not even your best friends."

"I'll try not to. G'bye."

"Thank you and give my love to Jean . . . I mean Mrs. Kerr."

In a like manner I managed to secure the cooperation of the Messrs. Taubman, Watts, Chapman, Nadel, and McClain. Only Robert Coleman required a personal visitation. A financial public relations man, he was aware of all the chicanery of the business. After a few hours in his office on lower Broadway, I convinced him that his participation would in no way jeopardize his standing in the financial community.

With my seven "phantom" critics in tow and sworn to secrecy, I proceeded to research the quotes, selecting the most laudatory phraseology from reviews of a few of Broadway's biggest hits. Then I prepared carefully worded statements for each of my new-found friends to sign granting permission to use their names and quotations in paid advertisements.

A pleasant week of previews was marred by a single recalcitrant. My John Chapman got up and left the St. James Theatre during the intermission one evening. As he passed me in the lobby, he growled, "I think it stinks."

Who needs him, I thought; the Manhattan phone book is full of John Chapmans.

As for the rest, they enjoyed the show immensely, much to my surprise. I suppose it was because the price was right. There was nothing wrong with our late evening suppers either; I was abundantly generous with Mr. Merrick's money.

One night, while sipping Scotch with the Taubmans and the Kerrs in the Oak Room, I was spotted by a colleague who came over to our table. When with a half smile I introduced my guests to him, he muttered something that sounded suspiciously like "Up yours," before withdrawing.

I accounted for this breach of etiquette by explaining that not even my closest colleagues were aware of our little caper. Taubman winced. A salesman of audio equipment in a Lexington Avenue shop, he said, "I hope I didn't spill the whole thing the other day."

Panic gripped me. "What happened?" I asked.

"Well, one of my customers is in show business," he replied. "I told him about your call and asked him what I should do. I wasn't sure if your invitation was on the level. He told me not to worry about it and to have a good time at the show."

"And your customer's name?" I inquired.

"Leland Hayward."

Hayward was a respected producer who occasionally joined Merrick in a theatrical venture. I silently prayed that he would leave town for a month or at least develop a severe case of laryngitis.

With everybody signed up, I reported to Merrick that phase one of his ingenious plan had been carried out successfully. Now we had to take another person into our confidence. We went to see Fred Golden, Merrick's account executive at the Blaine-Thompson Advertising Agency.

Merrick closed the door to Freddie's office, peering around first for possible eavesdroppers. Then he outlined the plot, demanding that blood oaths of secrecy be obtained from all agency personnel who would be involved in the mechanical preparation of the ad. "Don't submit the completed ad to the papers until the very last minute before insertion," he insisted. "I don't want the copy acceptance departments to have any time to study it carefully."

Our three great minds blended to come up with a headline: "7 OUT OF 7 ARE ECSTATICALLY UNANIMOUS ABOUT *SUBWAYS ARE FOR SLEEPING*." Not particularly clever or well-said, but not exactly soft-sell either. The remaining copy was to consist of the names and the quotes:

HOWARD TAUBMAN—"ONE OF THE FEW GREAT MUSICAL COMEDIES OF THE LAST THIRTY YEARS, ONE OF THE BEST OF OUR TIME. It lends lustre to this or any other Broadway season."

WALTER KERR—"WHAT A SHOW! WHAT A HIT! WHAT A SOLID HIT! If you want to be overjoyed, spend an evening with *Subways Are For Sleeping*. A triumph!"

JOHN CHAPMAN—"NO DOUBT ABOUT IT. *SUBWAYS ARE FOR SLEEPING* IS THE BEST MUSICAL OF THE CENTURY. Consider yourself lucky if you can beg or steal a ticket for *Subways Are For Sleeping* over the next few years."

JOHN MCCLAIN—"A FABULOUS MUSICAL. I LOVE IT. SOONER OR LATER

EVERYONE WILL HAVE TO SEE *SUBWAYS ARE FOR SLEEPING*."

RICHARD WATTS— "A KNOCKOUT, FROM START TO FINISH. THE MUSICAL YOU'VE BEEN WAITING FOR. IT DESERVES TO RUN FOR A DECADE."

NORMAN NADEL— "A WHOPPING HIT. RUN, DON'T WALK, TO THE ST. JAMES THEATRE. It's in that rare class of great musicals. Quite simply, it has everything."

ROBERT COLEMAN— "A GREAT MUSICAL. ALL THE INGREDIENTS ARE THERE. As fine a piece of work as our stage can be asked to give us."

A few days before the official opening, Freddie submitted a layout to Merrick, who thought it lacked a single element. In the interest of "integrity" he wanted it to include a photograph of each member of his personal critics' circle. A photographer was dispatched on a whirlwind tour of the Bronx, Manhattan, and New Jersey to shoot the portraits. Our critics had to admit they were enjoying the attention immensely.

The official opening night of *Subways Are For Sleeping* was filled with mixed emotions. The preview performances had gone so well that we began to harbor some faint hope that the show would be treated kindly by the real critics. At the same time, like children with a marvelous secret waiting to be shared, we wanted the gag ad to run.

The actual reviews were split down the middle. Chapman, Watts, and Coleman were affirmative. Taubman, Kerr, and McClain were negative. Nadel was on the fence, and only the slightest nudge would have made him drop on the negative side. Not even the ayes, however, were enthusiastic enough to deter us from our original course. Freddie was told to proceed as planned and to submit the ad to five papers for insertion on Thursday, January 4.

Late in the afternoon of January 3, Merrick, his general manager, Jack Schlissel, and I set up a night watch in Freddie's office. "Do you realize," he asked us, "that if all the papers run this ad, I'll be out twenty-five thousand dollars? It's worth it, isn't it? There's never been a more pointed comment on those boring quote ads. And who knows, maybe it'll help the show run longer."

As we savored what was to come, the evening wore on. We ran out of things to talk about, people to knock, show business jokes to tell. Then, at 7:30, the *Times* called to advise Freddie that they had caught on and would not run the ad. They considered it misleading. To protect the sanctity of the press in general, they had even alerted all the other papers. But it had been too late to catch the *Herald-Tribune*, which had already gone to press with its City Edition.

Freddie cajoled the man from the *Times*. "We make no claim that these seven people work for newspapers," he said. "We've even run their pictures so that there will be no mistaking them for the real critics. It's a clever comment, that's all. Where's your sense of humor?"

The *Times* wouldn't budge. But at least we had the first edition of the *Trib*. As soon as it was off the presses, Schlissel and I picked up an armful of copies. If nothing else, they'd be collector's items in the years to come.

Later we heard that the *Post* thought we had included the wrong photograph of Richard Watts. Our Watts was black; theirs was not. As they were replacing our photo with theirs, the call from the *Times* came in. The *Post* immediately killed the ad.

As a publicity stunt, however, the hoax was a huge success. It was reported throughout the world. The saga of Merrick's clever ruse appeared in *France Soir*, the *London*

Times, the *Stockholm Dagbladet,* and the *Tokyo Shimbun.* Within a few days, the *Trib* itself reran the ad, this time as editorial matter, together with an ad of their own creation that revealed what the actual critics had said. But they were not above pointing fun at themselves for falling victim to a splendid practical joke.

In its issue of January 12, 1962, *Time* reported: " . . . David Merrick has done it again. Last week, with a full-page ad that managed to run in an early edition of the New York *Herald-Tribune,* he perpetrated one of Broadway's most brazen jokes."

The *Time* article quoted Merrick's explanation for selecting his particular Richard Watts: "There isn't one critic who is a Negro, which I consider a violation of the Fair Employment Practices law. My group is more representative."

The reaction of the legitimate critics was mixed. John McClain wrote that it was "so original and funny, it warranted publication." Kerr, who found the show "limp," was not enchanted by Merrick's latest escapade. Taubman refused comment.

The Better Business Bureau sternly denounced Merrick's brainchild as "deceptive and confusing." When he learned of this, he said, "What is the Better Business Bureau? Something like the Diner's Club?"

Given a shot in the arm by all this publicity, *Subways Are For Sleeping* managed to survive until June, when dismal word-of-mouth finally caught up with it, and it came to the end of the line. But Merrick's reputation as a prankster was forever secure.

After the closing, he called me and said, "I've got an idea for the greatest publicity stunt in the history of the theatre. Want to hear it?"

Oh no, not again. But nothing in this world could keep him from telling me, so I dutifully said, "What is it, David?"

"It's an idea that's guaranteed to turn up long lines at the box office: *a great show that wins unanimous raves.*"

11

ᴄMerrick's Bay of Pigs

Everybody working on the show was confused, no one more so than I. (On any given day I would have been hard pressed to tell you its title.) It was a musical based on Truman Capote's short novel, *Breakfast at Tiffany's,* and on paper it looked like the blockbuster of the 1966-67 season. Merrick was the producer, Nunnally Johnson and Abe Burrows adapted it, Bob Merrill wrote the lyrics and music, and Burrows was the director. Mary Tyler Moore, fresh from a long run on the Dick Van Dyke television show, played Capote's popular heroine, Holly Golightly, and Richard Chamberlain abandoned his practice as TV's Dr. Kildare to be her co-star. (Capote rejected Merrick's offer to adapt the book himself, saying, "I don't function well in team sports.")

This all-star lineup impressed the theatregoing public. Without much urging, a great many entertainment-seekers mailed in their checks for tickets. Before we arrived in

Philadelphia and Boston, these engagements were completely sold out, and the New York advance sale had
passed the million-dollar mark.

To avoid comparison with the excellent film that had
been made with Audrey Hepburn, the show was first called
Holly Golightly, and under this title it opened in Philadelphia to a terrible panning. The consensus among the
Philadelphia critics was that it didn't measure up to the
movie, and that there wasn't a song in it comparable to
Johnny Mercer's "Moon River," written for the film.

But musicals are generally made during out-of-town
tryouts, so nobody panicked. It stood to reason that the
pros at work would be able to fix it before Broadway.

During the tryout the title was switched from *Holly Golightly* to *Breakfast at Tiffany's,* and it shifted back and
forth almost daily until I nearly went mad trying to keep
up with the changes in my ads and publicity copy.

Time reported that "in Philadelphia, Holly came off as
a tough fifty-dollar-a-shot hooker instead of a sweet fifty-
dollar-a-shot hooker. By the time the show reached Boston, Holly had become a nice young thing who might just
shack up with anybody for nothing."

The Boston press was unrelentingly harsh. Kevin Kelly
of the *Globe,* Merrick's old friend from *Subways Are For
Sleeping* days, now promoted to first-stringer, called it "a
multi-set disaster, a straightforward musical flop."

Understandably dissatisfied with the way things were
going, Merrick began to seek outside help. At the suggestion of a staff member, he approached Edward Albee, who
came to Boston to see several performances. It was a rather
unusual choice since Albee had no prior experience with
musicals, but he agreed to revise the script. "I'll probably
rewrite it completely," he said, "not because it's so terribly
bad, but because I have another approach—closer to Capote's original."

Capote, who up to now had been strangely quiet, commented, "I think it's very interesting. Albee is a friend of
mine. I'm curious to see what he'll do. He's got a very
interesting mind."

Merrick sought Burrows' approval to bring in Albee. Affably enough, Abe agreed. "Let's give it a try," he said. "He's not exactly a schlump." Burrows had run out of inspiration. Although he was certain that he wouldn't exactly be jailed for the show, directing and writing at the same time had gotten to be too much for him.

In show business it is said that the three most overrated things in the world are Japanese food, extramarital sex, and going out of town with a musical. Personally, I hate the first, am afraid of trying the second, and have been forced to do the third. Life with this show proved the veracity of that last claim. It was particularly brutal for the cast. While playing the Johnson-Burrows version at night, the actors spent the day rehearsing Albee's material. Burrows, however, slipped into a state of hopeless despair. He had to be replaced by Joseph Anthony, a veteran director. I must have spent a fortune of the production's money—ordering new printing and theatre signs. And still the New York advance sale increased. Word-of-mouth could not defeat this monster.

Nobody could tell much about the Albee version until it was on its feet in front of an audience. That opportunity came soon enough with the first preview on a Monday evening at the Majestic Theatre in New York. Apart from the Merrill score, the show, now set with the title *Breakfast at Tiffany's*, bore little resemblance to the pre-Broadway version; in fact it bore little resemblance to Capote's effective novella. Albee's Holly was a hard-bitten broad, and poor, sweet Mary Tyler Moore was in no way equipped for this interpretation.

Merrick wisely spent most of that initial preview hiding backstage. For the first time in my life I listened to an audience talk back to the actors. At one point, Mary Tyler Moore, having been knocked up by a random lover, said something to the effect that she'd better go see a doctor. "Better you should go see a lawyer and get out of this show," someone shouted from the rear of the orchestra. I slumped so deep in my seat that I've had back trouble ever since.

At the intermission I, too, sought refuge backstage, where I spied Merrick. "How do I get out of here alive?" he asked me. "Shave your moustache, David," I replied. "No one will ever recognize you."

The following evening's performance went about the same way. Unbelieving audiences, with fresh memories of the Audrey Hepburn film, were appalled. They walked out in droves. Merrick, however, had made up his mind that afternoon. He called me to his office and advised me that he was closing the show after the Wednesday evening preview. Through me he issued the following statement to the press:

> Rather than subject the drama critics and the theatregoing public—who invested one million dollars in advance sales—to an excruciatingly boring evening, I have decided to close. Since the idea of adapting *Breakfast at Tiffany's* for the musical stage was mine in the first place, the closing is entirely my fault and should not be attributed to the three top writers (Nunnally Johnson, Abe Burrows, and Edward Albee) who had a go at it.

Before the matinee on Wednesday, the closing notice was posted on the backstage bulletin board, abruptly ending employment for sixty-six people that night.

The press hailed Merrick as a man of forthright honesty. Speaking to reporters, he referred to the fiasco as "my Bay of Pigs." He emerged from the debacle a hero, a man who had refused to inflict shabby merchandise on an unsuspecting public. He was an American rarity.

Financially, the principal loser was Merrick himself, since he was far and away the largest investor. Later he was to tell the writer Dick Schaap that he thought President Lyndon Johnson could improve his image, too, by applying the Merrick tactic to the war in Vietnam. "It's a bad show," he suggested. "Fold it."

"You know," Merrick said to a writer from the *Boston Herald*, "this is the first time in the history of show business that a producer has had the integrity to close a boring show of his own before it opened. I saw it. It was a bore, so I gave them back their money. Those people who buy benefit tickets have to pay too much for an overpriced ticket, as it is, for charity. So I thought I'd be charitable and let them spend their money on one of my proven hits, like *Cactus Flower* or *Hello, Dolly!*"

Since his successes far outnumber his failures, Merrick is loaded. He was able to jest about this expensive fiasco. He told the columnist Earl Wilson, "I closed because Tiffany's, the jewelry outfit, promised to pay off the loss. Their competitor, Cartier's, wanted me to keep it open to damage Tiffany's."

The actors, however, took the closing much harder. John Gruen, then writing for that short-lived newspaper with the tripartite cognomen, the *World-Journal-Tribune*, visited backstage on the final night. He reported that Mary Tyler Moore wept as she took her bows. She told Gruen, "I am feeling all the emotions that you can imagine I must be feeling. All I can say now is that I want to be with my friends and share in some warm good-byes."

Richard Chamberlain said, "I thought Merrick was right to close the show. It just didn't work. But it was a marvelous experience for me. I've never been in a Broadway musical before, and I want to continue being in them. I thought everyone who worked on the show was wonderful. But there was not enough time to fix it."

The scars borne by Miss Moore and Mr. Chamberlain soon disappeared. She went on to greater triumphs in television, and today wouldn't accept all of Manhattan Island to return to the stage. Chamberlain went to England, where he learned from the bottom up how to handle classical roles, distinguishing himself in several Shakespearean productions, including *Hamlet*.

Later that season Merrick was speaking by phone to a friend who was a White House aide. Commiserating with the producer about the closing of *Breakfast at Tiffany's,* the government functionary remarked, "It must have been expensive."

Ever mindful of his elevated tax bracket, Merrick said, "That's all right. You're paying seventy-five percent of it."

12

Don't Fire 'til You See the Whites of Their Palms

Punctuality is an obsession with me. If I am as much as five minutes late for an appointment or a theatre curtain, I tend to go to pieces. You can imagine my hysteria, then, when my wife, youngest son, and I left for Washington by car at five o'clock on a Friday evening in December, 1967, to see the first preview of a brand-new David Merrick musical, the curtain on which was to rise at eight.

Washington is a boring five-hour drive from New York, and our departure had been delayed three hours by a series of seemingly endless office crises. "We should have flown down. There's no way we can make it now," I said as I jumped into the waiting car.

"Flying's expensive," said my wife, "and besides, it's nice to have the car for sightseeing the rest of the weekend. Don't be so uptight. It's only a preview. The show doesn't open until Monday."

"You're absolutely right, as always," I said, "but you

know how I hate to be late. What if Merrick asks me what I thought of the show? All I'll be able to say is that the curtain calls were terrific. Watching the first paid performance tells me a lot—like how long I'll be working."

The new Merrick production was called *Mata Hari*. It was about the exotic dancer accused and executed by the French for being a German spy in World War I. As we sped through the fields of oil refineries that dot the Jersey landscape, my wife asked me if I'd heard any word about the show. "It looks good," I replied. "At least that's what everybody told me during rehearsals. They say Minnelli's doing a wonderful job."

My reference was to Vincente, not Liza. He was the director of this opus, although he had not staged a Broadway musical in twenty-eight years. During that time he had directed many motion pictures, some of them first rate. He had also married Judy Garland, and fathered Liza.

One thing you knew for sure. *Mata Hari* couldn't possibly have a happy ending, not unless the writers messed around a little with history. It would have to wind up with an execution, and that is no way to end a Broadway musical. Leave 'em laughing, the pundits say. And how the hell are they gonna laugh at an execution?

To enact the role of Mata Hari, Merrick signed a Viennese actress, Marissa Mell—not too well known in the States, but extremely beautiful. Already he was monkeying with history. My limited research on the original Miss Hari, or Miss Mata, whatever she called herself, had produced a few old photographs. If the homely, fortyish, overweight woman posing coyly in a tassled bra was the famous femme fatale who persuaded French intelligence officers to open their files to her, then Marissa Mell could corrupt the entire French army, from Marshal Foch down to the lowest *poilu*.

On a previous trip to Washington to plant advance publicity on *Mata Hari* I had been advised that the first preview would be a gala benefit for the National Democratic

Women's Club. Adventuresome souls, these National Democratic Women. They weren't aware that they had something more to fear than fear itself.

We drove on without stopping, and it was 10:30 when we pulled into a parking garage next door to the National Theatre on E Street. "Let's go," I shouted, handing the key to an attendant. "We just might make the finale."

Entering the darkened theatre, we sat down in three empty seats in the last row. Before we could focus on what was happening onstage, the curtain lowered and the house lights went up.

"Damn it," I cursed. "We missed the whole thing."

The audience, however, did not applaud. Nor was there a single curtain call. "It must be a disaster," I said as I got up to look for someone working on the show. Spotting "Biff" Liff, Merrick's production manager, standing at the rear of the house, I ran over to him and asked, "What the hell's going on? Is it that bad?"

"Don't ask," he replied.

"Whattya mean 'don't ask,' " I said. "I just got here. Almost killed myself and my family driving down, only to miss the entire performance."

He looked at me quizzically. "You haven't missed the entire performance," he said. "That was just the end of the first act."

"Did you start on time?"

"Ten after eight."

"Then what's the problem, besides the fact that the show is badly in need of cutting?"

"Listen," he said, "I don't have the time to tell you all the things that are wrong. I have to go backstage. See you later."

I returned to my family to report that we were indeed fortunate; we'd be able to see the entire second act. "I'm not sure I'd call that fortunate," said my wife. "I've been listening to the comments around me and they're horrendous. Stick around and you'll get an earful. You'll also be able to see Lynda Bird Johnson draw a lucky program number for a door prize. If we're as fortunate as you say we are, maybe we'll win."

"Win what?" I asked.

"How do I know? We just got here. The woman sitting next to me said that Lynda Bird, who's up there in that box, will draw the number."

A follow-spot picked up the President's daughter, who, after a few inaudible remarks, reached into a large cardboard carton and announced the winning number.

"Do you know what the prize is?" I asked a distinguished-looking man who was standing in the aisle next to me.

"I would hope that it is permission to leave the theatre NOW," he replied hostilely. I never did learn what the prize was.

Once the second act had begun, the problems of *Mata Hari* were as apparent to me as they were to everyone else in that audience. The show was laborious and burdened with scenery that not only was uninteresting to look at, but also did not work properly. Mata Hari's ill-starred romance with the handsome but married French intelligence officer, Captain Henri LaFarge, was going as badly as the performance. LaFarge was being played by Pernell Roberts, who had recently left a secure job as one of the Cartwright brothers on "Bonanza." (Sometimes actors do the craziest things.)

LaFarge has been told that his sinuous paramour is using him to obtain military secrets. Torn with remorse and self-recrimination, he turns her in. Unable to face *her* fate, he leaves for a vacation at a mountain retreat in the French Alps. As he finishes a ballad about grief and loss, sung on a balcony overlooking a painted Alpine vista, the set must separate on cue, each half moving into the wings, to reveal a bleak courtyard where Mata will face the firing squad.

The set, however, became stuck. Violent attempts to move it nearly separated Roberts from his hairpiece. Finally, with no additional words to speak, or notes to sing, he took the line of least resistance. He vaulted the carved railing and walked offstage, his hands over his face as if that would make him invisible to the audience. The orchestra leader attempted to muffle the cries of backstage panic by conducting a medley of forgettable tunes from the show.

I suffered in silence, but the audience responded enthusiastically. For them these improvisations were the high point of the evening. Gales of laughter filled the National.

After an interminable wait, the set finally parted, and at last we were in the courtyard. Mata Hari was led in by a squad of riflemen and tied to a post. Now the orchestra switched to the "Marseillaise" as the officer in charge ordered the firing squad to the ready.

"Why the 'Marseillaise'?" my wife whispered.

I whispered back, "Because the authors believe that Mata Hari was innocent, that she was a French double agent unjustly accused and convicted."

"Oh, I see," she said. "Just another war atrocity."

A fusillade of shots followed the command to fire, and Miss Mell slumped at the stake. The strains of the "Marseillaise" became stronger as the officer drew his pistol to apply the *coup de grace*. A single shot, and Miss Mell slumped still farther.

As the curtain lowered, ever so slowly, the firing squad disappeared into the wings, leaving the forlorn figure of the world's most glamorous spy alone onstage, dead at the stake. Still the curtain came down, inches at a time. As the "Marseillaise" reached its climax, one of Miss Mell's hands appeared from behind her back, shook free from the rope around the wrist, and scratched her itching nose. Curtain.

By now every member of the audience was laughing uncontrollably. If it had not been close to one in the morning, they would have demanded an encore. I glanced at my teenage son. He was fast asleep.

The usual post-opening confusion prevailed backstage where I sought out Merrick. "It's a monumental disaster," he said, using one of his favorite expressions. "I don't see how it can be fixed."

"What are you going to do, David?" I asked.

"Why, close it, of course," he replied, regarding me as some kind of idiot for asking such a question.

"Isn't there any hope?" I asked.

"I heard the audience roaring out there. It just might work if we played the whole show as a comic farce. Leave all the fluffs in. I'm going to suggest it to the writers and Minnelli."

That night, as we drove to our Washington hotel, my wife turned to me and inquired, "Did Merrick ask you what you thought?"

"He didn't have to," I replied. "He knows it's a turkey."

"What was so important about being on time? The ship was sinking. Another rat on board wouldn't have helped."

"Thanks a lot," I said. "Would you have wanted to miss that extraordinary performance? The next time you see this show it's liable to be a farce comedy."

"What would you call it tonight?" she said.

Merrick discussed his new concept with the authors and the director, but they were appalled by it. Refusing to buck their organized resistance, he applied his own *coup de grace* to *Mata Hari*. He closed it three weeks later, at the end of the Washington engagement.

The authors, however, were a persistent lot. They refused to surrender. They wanted their show done in New York so badly that they themselves produced it off-Broadway a year later under the title, *Ballad for a Firing Squad*. The critics hated it, and it closed after seven performances.

13

The Rat
in the Generator

The phone call was from the drama department of the *New York Times.* A secretary said she was calling for Stanley Kauffmann, the new drama critic appointed midway in the 1965-66 season. Mr. Kauffmann wanted two tickets for the final preview of *Philadelphia, Here I Come* in lieu of the usual opening-night tickets. I said I'd get back to her.

Decisions on matters like these are best left to the producer. I therefore relayed the conversation to David Merrick, who said, "Go ahead and send him the tickets, but include a note."

"Saying what?" I asked.

"Just 'AT YOUR PERIL,' and you can put it over my signature," he replied.

" 'AT YOUR PERIL'? What does that mean?"

"I don't know yet," he said. "I'll think of something."

Kauffmann's request was not unexpected. He had succeeded Howard Taubman as drama critic of the *Times*

only six weeks before, and had already created consterna-
tion in the theatre community. A scholarly man who had
written criticism for *The New Republic,* among other jour-
nals, Kauffmann wanted to change the "system." He did
not want to play the game by the old rules. Without prior
daily newspaper experience, he wanted more than the usual hour and a half in which to write his review. He made
it known that he would attend preview performances
rather than the official opening nights. He was quoted as
saying, "A play that took ten years to write and a year to
produce deserves more than a fifty-minute review."

Clifton Daniel, then managing editor of the *Times,*
called the other daily drama critics in an attempt to elicit
support for the Kauffmann modus operandi. John Chapman of the *News* said, "I think I'll just go along as I always have and cover the opening."

Richard Watts of the *Post* favored the status quo. "I believe in the white-hot impact of the play," he commented.
"Besides, a morning-paper critic tried it many years ago
and it was a great flop."

John McClain of the *Journal-American* admitted that
were he forced to attend a preview, he would no doubt
wait until the last minute anyway before sitting down to
the typewriter. Another scornfully said that with twenty-
four hours at his disposal, he could write a sequel to *War
and Peace.*

Walter Kerr, then reviewing for the *Herald-Tribune,* log-
ically termed the *Times*'s proposal "a complete change in
the present system, necessitating the approval and cooperation of all newspapers as well as producers."

Most producers, however, objected. Harold Prince said
that he was "unalterably opposed. I hardly feel that the
critic has the right to see a preview while the producer is
still making changes in the show right up to opening
night."

Prince's protest was seconded by the League of New
York Theatres, the Dramatists' Guild, the Society of Stage
Directors and Choreographers, actors, stagehands, a few

press agents, and a couple of orange juice hawkers.

Baited into offering his opinion of preview coverage, and critics in general, David Merrick stated, "I don't think it will help them. I don't think they know what they're doing anyway. My opinion is that it won't make any difference whatsoever, even if they cover seven nights in a row. They can attend as many performances as possible —previews, openings, post-views. So far as I am concerned, they can also attend rehearsals."

At the time of Kauffmann's ascendance to the critic's chair at the *Times*, Merrick was preparing *Philadelphia, Here I Come*, an Irish play by the as-yet-unknown Brian Friel. Irish plays traditionally stir little advance interest among Broadway theatregoers. And this one had no "names" in the cast. Merrick realized that its commercial fate would be decided solely by the critics.

Merrick had repeatedly vilified Taubman in print and on the air. At a chance meeting a few weeks before, Taubman introduced Merrick to his successor, saying, "Mr. Kauffmann, I'd like you to meet David Merrick—the enemy."

Philadelphia, Here I Come opened quietly in Philadelphia, where it was warmly received by the critics, and steadily built an audience. It was a touching and effective play deserving of every chance of success on Broadway, but we realized that no great amount of pre-opening advertising would pay off. We just had to wait, and pray for good notices.

Only two previews, priced from two to four dollars, were scheduled before the Wednesday evening premiere. Kauffmann had his tickets to the Tuesday preview, along with Merrick's note, but he never bothered to inquire as to the meaning of its ominous message. Nor had the producer told me what it meant.

On Tuesday morning, however, Merrick asked me to come to his office. "I've made up my mind," he said. "Kauffmann must be forced to attend the opening night and not the preview."

"How do we arrange that?" I asked.

"I'm cancelling the preview," he replied, "and I've instructed the box office to stop selling tickets for tonight —without telling them why. No point in inconveniencing the public."

"Do I call the *Times* and tell them?"

"Of course not. It's got to look like a last-minute thing. Let Kauffmann come to the theatre and then tell him the performance has been cancelled because of technical difficulties."

"Technical difficulties? What kind?"

"Just explain that a rat got caught in the generator during the early evening," he said, "and none of the lights at the Helen Hayes Theatre are working: We'll offer refunds or exchanges to those who bought seats."

"If you say so, David," I said, barely concealing my disapproval.

"What's the matter?" he asked.

"I don't like lying to the press," I said.

"Then blame me," he countered. "Other producers complain, but I'm doing something about it."

At 7:30 I reluctantly headed for the Helen Hayes, where I posted a sign alongside the box office to the effect that tonight's performance was cancelled. I then hunted up the house electrician and asked him to turn off the marquee lights. Now all I had to do was wait for Kauffmann. He arrived close to curtain time. When he heard my story, he voiced his skepticism, and headed back to his office. I am not a convincing fibber, but as far as I was concerned, the matter was closed, and I went home.

Later that night I received a call from Sam Zolotow, the tenacious drama columnist of the *Times*. He reported that his paper was planning a front-page story about the incident. I was surprised, since it would only serve to embarrass the critic. Sam asked me for the real reason behind the cancellation, but I stuck to the original fable.

The next morning the *Times* did run a front-page story. The headline read: "The Dark Preview or 'At Your

Peril.' " My memo to Kauffmann was reproduced in the story. Zolotow pointed out that "the lack of marquee lights was attributed to the generator failure, but the lobby lights were on."

Time magazine conjectured, "Was this an ambush, calculated to embarrass the *Times*'s critic? No. Merrick's press agent explained: a generator was out of order. That seemed funny: although the marquee was blacked out, the lobby lights were blazing."

On request I provided a pair of opening-night tickets to Kauffmann. The premiere went off as scheduled. *Philadelphia, Here I Come* was embraced by every critic with the notable exception of the man from the *Times*. But the show, with its new-found fame, became a hit, and enjoyed a long and profitable run.

Merrick wasn't finished with Stanley Kauffmann by a long shot. On a subsequent trip to London, he ambled into a bookshop and spotted a copy of a tawdry sex novel entitled *The Philanderer*. It had been written some years back by his old friend, Kauffmann, and was out of print in the States.

The Philanderer had been the subject of an obscenity trial in England that found in its favor, but its purple prose could not have enhanced its author's reputation. *Time* quoted a short passage: " 'Darling,' she whispered. How lazy a woman's first words after love-making; how husky and bare."

Merrick bought up every copy of *The Philanderer* that the London bookstore had in stock, had them shipped to New York, and mailed eighty-nine copies to critics and editors all over the United States, and ten copies to the top men at the *Times*. (He kept one for himself.) Each was accompanied by a small memo that read, "Compliments of David Merrrickk," the triple "r" and double "k" being a barbed comment on Kauffmann's spelling of his name. "If I'm lucky," said the producer, "I'll get arrested for sending unseemly matter through the mails."

Whether it was his pedantic approach to criticism, or

the merry pranks of Merrick that finished him off, I am not certain, but Stanley Kauffmann did not last out the year as drama critic of the New York *Times*. He was replaced by Walter Kerr, who became available when the *Herald-Tribune* went out of business.

It should be noted, however, that today, in his position as the Sunday critic for the *Times*, Kerr frequently asks for—and is granted—permission by producers to attend preview performances of new productions. So did Clive Barnes, who also covers dance and occasionally ran into conflicting dates.

From time to time Stanley Kauffmann still reviews plays for *The New Republic*. He attends second-night performances. No doubt *The New Republic* deadlines are more to his liking.

14

I Bombed in
Boston and Philadelphia

The switchboard operator looked up as I entered my office whistling a tune from a long-forgotten musical. "My, but you're the happy one today," she said.

"Sweetie," I said, "I'm always happy when I sign a contract to handle a new play."

"That's wonderful—a new play. What's it called?" she asked.

"*Isle of Children*," I replied.

"What a nice title—*I Love Children*," she said, enunciating each word clearly.

I saw no point in correcting her. Besides, her title was better than the playwright's.

Isle of Children had been written by Robert L. Joseph, the same Robert L. Joseph who had produced *King Lear* and *My Darlin' Aida*. Its central character was a thirteen-year-old girl of exceptional intelligence and sensitivity who is dying of an incurable heart ailment. Her father, a writer, attempts to soften her last days by creating a world of fantasy around his doomed daughter. Her mother, somewhat more practical, goes from doctor to doctor seeking someone who can restore the child's health. Naturally this creates conflict in the family, but eventually the parents become reconciled to the inevitable, as does the perceptive child, who comes to realize that her brief life span will leave unfulfilled all her good intentions.

The theme of imminent death is recurrent in both plays and films. It is guaranteed to effect much twisting of handkerchiefs and shredding of tissues, but it does not necessarily assure box office success. I always create a little scene in my mind that frequently tells me if a play is going to go with the Broadway patron. In this case it went something like this:

> WIFE: Let's go to the theatre tonight.
> HUSBAND: Whaddya wanna see?
> WIFE: *Isle of Children.*
> HUSBAND: What's it about?
> WIFE: The death of a little girl.
> HUSBAND: Let's watch television.

The news that Patty Duke had signed to play the ill-fated young woman and that Jules Dassin would return from exile in Europe to direct *Isle of Children* was a plus. A few seasons back Miss Duke had made an electrifying stage debut as Helen Keller in William Gibson's *The Miracle Worker*. Without uttering a word, she was able to portray the early anguish and frustration of this extraordinary character whose inner resolve and intelligence were eventually brought out by her teacher and companion, Anne Macy Sullivan, played by Anne Bancroft.

In a pre-opening interview with the Boston critic, Elliot Norton, Joseph stated with sincere conviction: "This is no child actress. This is a beautiful spirit. This is a great actress to rank with the best we have ever had. Whether my play is good or bad, this is what will come of it. Her greatness!"

Dassin was one of the victims of Hollywood witch-hunts of the McCarthy era. Ten years earlier, he had fled to Europe as a political refugee with a modest reputation as a director. Now he was returning to his homeland as one of the most successful directors in motion pictures with such films as *Never on Sunday, He Who Must Die,* and *Rififi* to his credit. His romance with the outspoken Greek star of *Never on Sunday,* Melina Mercouri, was described in great detail by the gossip columns and fan magazines.

Because I believe that every show should have a point of view in its promotional concept, I strained to develop a theme for the advertising campaign of *Isle of Children,* preferably one that would conceal its subject matter. There I had tradition to back me up. Legitimate-theatre advertising tends to tell very little about the play it is selling. Apart from the obligatory billing and perhaps an eye-catching piece of art, the rest has to do with business—the dates, prices, theatre address, and phone number. Invariably, the play's plot is overlooked.

I found myself doodling slogans, some of them as foolish as "The Heartwarming Story of the Death of a Noble Young Child, Directed by a Victim of Hollywood's Years of Fear," or "If You Loved Patty Duke in *The Miracle Worker,* You'll Pray for Her in *Isle of Children.*"

One doodle, however, struck me as funny and perhaps even eye-catching. I grabbed the phone and called Bob Joseph, who shared my appreciation of the absurd. "Bob, remember when Garbo made her first talkie?" I asked.

"Of course," he said, "I was going on four at the time and had seen every one of her silent films from the time I was one. What about it?"

"Didn't the ads read 'Garbo Speaks'?"

"No, no, no," he replied. "You're thinking of the time she made her first comedy, *Ninotchka,* and the ads said, 'Garbo laughs'."

"I think you're right," I said. "Okay, so forget Garbo. But what I want to do is run a line that reads, 'Patty Duke Speaks'."

"Not on my show you won't."

"Please, just let me try it in Boston. If the press ridicules it, or if it has no effect on the public, I can always drop it before we open in New York."

He agreed, reluctantly, and my catch phrase did manage to generate a little business in Boston. After the curtain fell on opening night there, I visited the papers and picked up copies of the reviews. The critics noted that Patty Duke did indeed speak for the first time on a stage. They just weren't taken with the words she had to speak. Norton's review in *The Boston Post* began encouragingly enough, then he took it all back by writing: "Until the final scene of the final act, *Isle of Children* is a lovely, tender, touching play about a rare and exquisite child, a girl of 14, who is incurably ill. The play falls to pieces when the author resorts to fumbling fantasy in an attempt to create a final resolution of the story."

Elinor Hughes of the *Herald* failed to see anything at all in the play, calling it "talky, disorganized and bewildering." In the *Globe*, Kevin Kelly was even less complimentary. He commented: "At one point in *Isle of Children,* a grimly cheerful mother takes a vase of plastic roses to the sickroom of her daughter, a girl of 13 who is soon to die. The little girl raises herself from her bed, like a wilted Violetta, touches the flowers, and says with acrid sophistication: 'Don't they know they've had it? At least I'll outlive something around here!' But since the roses—like the play—are glossy plastic, the real threat is whether the evening will hold out long enough to give the poor kid a decent wake. Mr. Joseph's little girl is brave, defiant, poetically noble and patently incredible. It's a desperate evening."

Variety summed it up succinctly: " . . . it will have limited audience appeal."

After absorbing these brickbats, Joseph urged me to dispense with my smirky advertising slogan, but I had already begun to use it as the focal point of my campaign.

In an interview I arranged for her with the *Herald-Tribune*, Miss Duke had stated: "I don't know what it's like to talk on the stage. It'll be fun to see." Now that we knew it wasn't going to be much fun, I would have to switch gears. But I did not know what else we had to sell.

It was getting too hot for me in the Boston kitchen, so heeding Harry Truman's sage advice, I got out. Frustrated and concerned, I packed my bags, and in the early morning hours escaped to Philadelphia, where David Merrick was preparing a new musical entitled, *I Can Get It For You Wholesale*, based on Jerome Weidman's novel about the odyssey of a heel in the garment trade.

Merrick was concerned about the lack of audience for the forthcoming Saturday night preview. "Paper the house," he instructed me. "Take all the remaining orchestra seats and get them into the right hands. We haven't sold that much anyway."

"How about my distributing them to members of the International Ladies Garment Workers' Union?" I asked. "They should love it, and they'll identify with the show's Jewish texture."

He okayed my idea, and I placed a call to the business agent of the ILGWU's Philadelphia local. "Can you use six hundred free tickets for your members to see this Saturday's preview of *I Can Get It For You Wholesale?*" I inquired.

"I could use six thousand," he replied. "I remember reading the book. Very true to life."

"Okay," I said, "send over for them. Just give them to the workers—cutters, trimmers, buttonhole makers, and the like."

Came Saturday night and I was in the lobby of the Shubert to see the audience arrive. In the following half hour I watched my invited ILGWU-ers enter the house, and died a little with each one. When Merrick arrived he saw the anguish on my face. "What fell apart?" he asked.

"Everything," I replied. "I've just seen six hundred

Puerto Rican garment workers going into the theatre. I didn't realize that the ethnic balance of the ILGWU had changed in the past twenty years."

Merrick scowled at me, his coal-black eyes emitting sparks of fury. "They'll hate it, and I can thank you for that," he said.

I could only agree with him. "It's just not my week," I said lamely, and started to walk out of the lobby.

"Where are you going?" he asked.

"I can't bear to watch," I said. "I'll be in the bar next door."

"I think you ought to stay and suffer with the rest of us," he insisted.

The start of the performance had to be delayed a few minutes while the ushers sorted out the audience. My amigos, unfamiliar with legitimate-theatre procedures, had seated themselves where it suited them best, unmindful that each ticket bore a specific location. A tactful house manager straightened things out, averting a few pitched battles in the process, and the show began.

The curtain of *I Can Get It For You Wholesale* rises on "a series of vignettes depicting New York City's garment center at the height of a busy day in 1937." Various garment-center types—shipping clerks, handcart pushers, models, sewing-machine operators, and cutters are seen at their respective chores. Polite applause greeted these identifiable activities. Then, as picket signs appeared and a strike scene developed, murmurs of excitement ran through the house. Cheers went up as a scab was being assaulted by a group of strikers. It was a vibrant opening for this musical, but after that we were in trouble.

Recognition soon evaporated into mystification as words like *schlemiel, blintzes,* and *halvah* popped up in the dialogue.

But it was not so much the show's language (the authors had minimized the Yiddish words) or inflection, but rather a lack of sympathy for its brassy, venal anti-hero, played by a young actor named Elliott Gould, that caused the audience to react with indifference. It was perfectly able to grasp the meaning of a song entitled "Eat a Little Something," sung by Lillian Roth as a pushy Jewish mother (there must be pushy Puerto Rican mothers), or an onstage bar mitzvah party that opened the second act. But the Puerto Ricans—and just about everybody else—had nobody to root for. They stayed until the end, however, clapped a little, and left the Shubert much quieter than they'd been on arrival, unaware, I'm sure, that they had just witnessed the birth of a major new star in the girl who played Gould's secretary, Barbra Streisand.

Isle of Children and *I Can Get It For You Wholesale* opened on Broadway in March, 1962, within six days of each other. John McClain's review of the Joseph play in the *Journal-American* made me cringe. It began: " 'Patty Duke Speaks!' blared the press releases heralding the arrival in a new play of the young star who remained speechless throughout *The Miracle Worker*. Well, the new play is *Isle of Children* by Robert L. Joseph and it opened last night at the Cort Theatre. They weren't kidding when they said Miss Duke speaks: it is the understatement of the semester. She never stops."

The remaining notices ran from mildly favorable (Taubman of the *Times* wrote: " . . . a brave try at a delicate, elusive theme") to devastating (Watts of the *Post*: "depressing, monotonous and endlessly given to tedium"). Walter Kerr, dismissing the play as "a moody and somewhat self-conscious one-tone poem striking again and again the doleful note of a child's impending death," reserved his praise for Miss Duke. "Before they start tearing down any more New York theatres, they'd better hold one out," he wrote. "One of these days they're going to need it to name after Patty Duke."

Kerr was no better prophet than Bob Joseph in his appraisal of Miss Duke's future in the theatre. The play ran but eleven performances and Miss Duke never again appeared on the Broadway stage. Nor have her occasional film appearances fulfilled their expectations.

Wholesale fared somewhat better. Its critical reception was also widely divergent, from Kerr's paraphrase of a Harold Rome song in the show, "Momma, Momma, Momma, what a good solid show," to McClain's "Even at retail, it's no bargain." It ran for 300 performances. And Elliott Gould and Barbra Streisand fell in love with each other, married, and, as we all know, did *not* live happily ever after.

15

Starlight, Starfright

I admit to being star-struck—but only from a professional point of view. Since I believe that a press agent is only as good as what he sells, I, like my competitors, tended to look extraordinarily skillful when representing a production whose cast was headed by a star of magnitude. It was then that I was able to take sweeping bows as the media clamored for interviews and the public responded at the box office.

"If you've got a big star, you're just an order taker," a noted director once told me. While I resented his chilling put-down, I had to admit that he was partially right. With a big star, there would be no 3:00 A.M. calls from a nervous producer demanding to know why the advance sale in New Haven or Philadelphia was meager, or why he hadn't read reams of copy about his show in the newspapers.

The star vehicle renders all of these things unto a producer, as well as such other benefits as swift financing of his show and a possible box-office hedge against poor notices for the script.

Occasionally this formula fails. It depends on the caliber of the star. Any theatre buff is able to point to innumerable star-studded misfires, so monumentally cumbersome that they were beyond salvation. But frequently the star manages to triumph over mediocrity when an adoring public chooses to ignore rotten reviews.

A true box-office star should sell tickets regardless of the quality of the play. There are a handful of these from whom a reading of the Manhattan telephone book would turn out eager ticket buyers.

I have worked with many great stars and have nothing but fond remembrances of most of these transient associations. But it took Lucille Ball and Carol Burnett, two of the biggest, to teach me that under the best of circumstances, security in the theatre is nevertheless elusive.

The Misses Ball and Burnett have a few things in common. Both are exceptionally talented comediennes. Both have enjoyed their greatest successes on television. Both appeared on the Broadway musical stage in lightweight vehicles in the early 1960s, and both, I am sure, would today be loath to discuss their respective theatre experiences.

Lucille Ball chose for her debut on the New York stage a musical called *Wildcat* about a woman oil-driller, by N. Richard Nash, of *Rainmaker* fame. (It rained at the end of that one; this one gushed.) Cy Coleman and Carolyn Leigh wrote a score that produced one standard, "Hey, Look Me Over," forever after an anthem for football marching bands. *Wildcat* was produced by Nash and Michael Kidd, also the director and choreographer of this opus.

There was every good reason for Lucille Ball to do a Broadway show. Her marriage to Desi Arnaz had collapsed, bringing to an end their tremendously popular TV series, "I Love Lucy." Desi and Lucy had become big business; they owned their own film studio, the old RKO lot.

She believed that she had to escape Hollywood for a while.

It required four huge vans to bring "all the things I love" from Miss Ball's Beverly Hills and Palm Springs homes to fill and furnish her newly rented, seven-room, terraced apartment in the East Sixties. While in rehearsal for *Wildcat*, she told the Hollywood columnist Sheilah Graham, "I brought all the terrace furniture, five TV sets, a piano that was sitting out there doing nothing, the toys for my daughter, Lucie, little Desi's bongo drums, all my paintings, and all my books. Plus a limousine with chauffeur, and a big package of courage."

She justified the move by further stating, "I like a challenge. I've always wanted to be on the Broadway stage. It's a new medium for me, my first time on Broadway. Sure I'm scared and I get butterflies when I think of opening night. But I'm also excited about it. I chose *Wildcat* because it's close to the character I play in 'I Love Lucy.' "

Nobody worked harder during rehearsals than Lucille Ball. She was the complete professional—cooperative, cheerful, and totally attentive. The supporting cast and production staff adored her, and I numbered myself among her most ardent admirers. Our relationship was easy and comfortable, and unlike most Hollywood stars, who are afflicted with a touch of paranoia, she did not regard my presence as an intrusion on her privacy and energy. She trusted me and did not beg off a single interview that I arranged for her.

I looked forward to my daily visits to the theatre. Lucy's dressing room was a place of laughter. If you heard a joke, you'd save it up to tell her, and she, in turn, would have one to tell you. We used to try to top each other with clichés from Western films. I would enter and say, "Mornin', Miss Lucy. Goin' inta town?"

"Yup," she would reply. "When are ya comin' to fetch me?"

Or when I would arrive at her apartment and little Desi was practicing his bongos, I'd remark, "No need to worry, Miss Lucy, 'til the drums stop."

She'd come back with: "I know. They'll attack as soon as the sun comes up."

A sold-out Philadelphia tryout engagement preceded the New York premiere of *Wildcat* on December 16, 1960. It was apparent that whatever its shortcomings as musical theatre, *Wildcat* would triumph in the end because of the presence of its star. Nobody panicked even when the opening had to be postponed for a day because the scenery, en route from Philadelphia to New York in eight trailer trucks, was snowbound on the Jersey Turnpike somewhere between New Brunswick and Newark. A briefly discussed plan to move the scenery by helicopter, with Lucy aboard, was rejected as impractical by our hard-pressed general managers, Joe Harris and Ira Bernstein.

It was easy for the critics to praise the star, but difficult for them to say anything good about her show. Richard Watts reported in the *Post:* "It is good to see the handsome, talented, and vital Lucille Ball on the Broadway stage. It would be even better to see her in a good show."

Howard Taubman wrote in the *Times:* "Everybody wanted to love Lucille Ball, but her show didn't make it easy. Don't you care, Miss Ball. They all still love Lucy— and you, too."

Wildcat stepped immediately into the hit class, selling out at all performances, and Lucy worked herself into a frazzle trying to please her public. Daily she added to the show some hilarious *shtick* that she had perfected over the years in television. Audiences left the Alvin Theatre happy in the knowledge that they had been well entertained.

Eight performances a week, however, began to take their toll on the star. And less than two months after the opening, I was obliged to inform the press that *Wildcat* would suspend for two weeks because Lucille Ball was fighting a losing battle against a virus infection, and on doctor's orders, had gone to Miami Beach to recover.

When Lucy returned from Florida, she was no longer the cheerful woman of the early rehearsal days. Doing the same thing night after night was not as stimulating, she'd learned, as filming a new script on television each week. She was depressed, and wanted desperately to return to California.

On a clear, cool night in early April, Lucy, eager for someone to hear her troubles, invited me to go for a long walk with her. Her chauffeur dropped us on Riverside Drive somewhere near Grant's Tomb and we began to stroll, with the limousine following slowly behind. She hated the boredom of the show. She was exhausted. She felt uncomfortable in New York.

I sympathized, but offered no advice. What she wanted to hear was that it was perfectly all right for her to leave the show. I didn't think the producers would care much for my telling her that.

On May 6, her divorce from Desi Arnaz became final, after nineteen years of marriage. At a Wednesday matinee later that month, Lucy fainted onstage and was unable to continue. Was it more than a coincidence?

A few days later I received a large envelope from her. It contained a color photograph of herself on which was inscribed a foreboding message: "Harvey—Please come fetch me before it's too late. Love, Lucy." I knew then that *Wildcat* would close. And after struggling through a few more poorly attended performances with the understudy, it did just that, on June 3.

To leave the door open a little, I announced that the show would "suspend" for nine weeks because of the star's need for recuperation from exhaustion. But nothing would bring Lucille Ball back to Broadway once she had escaped. *Wildcat* went down in the books as just another flop. It never ran long enough to earn back its investment and it lost more than $300,000—all belonging to the show's sole backer, Desilu Productions.

Jack Gaver, a writer for United Press International, called the Carol Burnett caper "a case unique among all of the odd things that have happened on Broadway." An exaggeration, perhaps, but he said it, I didn't.

It all started innocently enough when Lester Osterman and Jule Styne, the composer, got together to produce an original musical called *A Girl to Remember.* Betty Comden and Adolph Green were writing the book and lyrics, and Styne, the music. George Abbott, just turned seventy-five, was engaged to direct. The show was to star Carol Burnett—then a burgeoning television personality— as a clumsy Broadway hoofer who, through mistaken identity, is picked for Hollywood stardom.

Characterized by the *Times* as "an interesting hybrid of one part 'American-as-apple-pie-girl-next-door'—a veritable pandowdy of wholesomeness—and one part amiable klutz," Miss Burnett confessed to the interviewer, "There's no doubt that theatre is the prestige medium. It's a bigger challenge to a performer. And doing eight shows a week is exhausting in some ways, exciting in others. You get the chance to experiment."

I announced the salient facts about *A Girl to Remember* to the theatre world and then I waited, and waited . . . and waited. I must have waited a year and a half before the money was raised, the script and score were completed, and the show was ready to go. Or at least I thought it was ready to go.

During that time, Carol did not twiddle her thumbs. She kept adding to her admirers through repeated appearances on the Garry Moore television show. It was only a question of time before she had her own TV show.

In the winter of 1962, Osterman advised me that his production would open on November 23, 1963, at the Mark Hellinger Theatre. Preparations continued through the rest of that winter and well into the spring. Several supporting actors were signed, as well as most of the singing chorus. Designers were commissioned, advertising was planned, dates were allocated to theatre party groups, a major record company agreed to do the original cast album. A serene air of optimism prevailed.

That feeling was short-lived. Early in June, a worried Lester Osterman called me. "You won't believe this," he said, "but the show's off until May of next year. Burnett's pregnant."

"Pregnant?" I yelled in shock. "By whom?"

"Her husband, of course," he replied.

I had forgotten that a few months earlier, Carol had married a television producer named Joe Hamilton, the father of eleven children by his first wife. Rehearsals, Lester said, could probably start in March, 1964.

"What about an abortion?" I asked.

"Her husband won't buy that," said Lester. "He's Catholic, I think."

"Terrific," I said. "He doesn't believe in abortion, but he believes in divorce?"

My engines had been all revved up, and now I was being told to go back to the hangar. Breathlessly, I released the information about Carol's confinement to an unsuspecting world of theatregoers, embellishing my announcement with some pertinent statistics: $1,000,000 in group sales was being returned, twenty Equity contract holders would each receive a two-week salary settlement in lieu of steady work, the Hellinger Theatre would be paid a nonrefundable $20,000 rental guarantee, and some $6,000 would be required for additional miscellaneous expenses incurred by the postponement. Miss Burnett's baby was going to be expensive—for Osterman and Styne.

During the gestation period, the show's title was changed from *A Girl to Remember* to *The Idol of Millions,* and finally to *Fade Out—Fade In.* Perhaps it should have remained *A Girl to Remember.*

In January Carol gave birth, and two months later, the picture of rosy good health, she reported for rehearsals, a bit reluctantly, it should be said, since the astronomical fees being offered her by the networks made Broadway inconsequential by comparison. Certainly she no longer needed the show as a steppingstone.

Rehearsals and the pre-Broadway engagement were, from my viewpoint, successful and pleasantly uneventful. My relationship with Miss Burnett was not as warm as the one I enjoyed with Lucille Ball. She tolerated me politely, and that was good enough. *Fade Out—Fade In* was a slightly better show than *Wildcat*. It provided its star with funnier material. It opened at the Hellinger on May 26, 1964, to mixed notices, but it became a solid hit, soon surpassing the box office records achieved by *My Fair Lady* at the same theatre.

In mid-June an abdominal ailment sidelined Carol for a few performances, and her understudy, Carolyn Kemp, took over. Although the producers had had the good sense to take out an insurance policy to cover Carol's absences, it paid them only $2,500 nightly, hardly enough to make up for the refunds.

In July, forewarned that their star would require a week off for minor surgery, the producers secured the services of Betty Hutton, a Hollywood luminary in limbo. They wanted to offer ticketholders a "name" as a replacement. Nevertheless, business that week slumped alarmingly.

Carol's appearances in *Fade Out—Fade In,* following her return from the operation, were sporadic. Claiming that "a very serious neck and back injury," incurred five years earlier, had been aggravated in July when a cab in which she was riding stopped short, she was ordered by her doctors (you and I have a doctor; a star and an ex-president have doctors) to spend most of every day in traction. The producers acceded to a request that her most difficult numbers in the show be curtailed, but they voiced skepticism about her ailment.

In late August, Carol missed another five performances because of the neck injury. Her absence resulted in more refunds.

Osterman and Styne's skepticism increased in mid-September when it was announced by Bob Banner Productions, a television producing firm, that their star had been signed to appear simultaneously on a new TV variety series entitled "The Entertainers," to be produced by her husband, Joe Hamilton. "I've missed the tube," she told Val Adams, the *Times*'s television columnist. "Television is my first love. It makes me furious when I hear television called the illegitimate child of show business."

Carol admitted that she had asked to be released from *Fade Out—Fade In*, but denied a rumor that she had offered a huge sum to buy up her contract. Osterman and Styne, however, admitted privately that her manager had proposed a $500,000 settlement, which they were forced to refuse when the authors objected. After the Hutton experience, they were also aware that their show was Burnett's, and that a replacement star wasn't feasible. In turn, they sought an injunction to prohibit Carol's television appearances.

Battle lines were rapidly being consolidated as each party engaged high-powered legal advisors. The producers retained Theodore Kheel; Miss Burnett hired Edward Costikyan.

The most explosive salvo yet was fired by Carol when, on October 13, she issued a statement that she must immediately cease all professional activity and enter a hospital for treatment of her back and neck. The doctors had recommended an indefinite period in traction, according to her personal press agent.

Four days later, she was admitted to the Hospital for Joint Diseases. Camera bulbs flashed on her arrival at the hospital entrance. Osterman and Styne asked a logical question: when would she be able to return? They received no definitive answer. "We'll run the show as long as we can," Osterman said with feigned determination. "If we can't, we will store the production pending her recovery. We say that she can't work in any other medium until she fulfills her contract with us."

Headlining Mitzi Welch, a new understudy, *Fade Out—Fade In* limped along to ever dwindling grosses until November 14, when, in the face of financial disaster, it was forced to close.

In reply to another request from the producers for the date of her return, Carol, now out of the hospital, wrote: "I have no idea when, if ever, I can return to the type of physical activity I was doing before I went into the hospital—simply because the doctors themselves do not know. I am sorry I got sick. I am sorry the play had to close because I was sick. I am sorry you don't think I'm sick."

Aware that she owed an explanation to the cast, Carol sent a message that was posted on the backstage bulletin board: "Just wanted to let you know how sorry I am about the whole mess. Someday, when it is all over, I'd like to tell all of you and the public about the producers and their play." She claimed that a doctor recommended by Osterman had warned her in September that she "would risk serious injury if I didn't cease all activity." She said she had no idea when she could go back to work and "that is why I could not let our producers know."

Osterman and Styne promptly brought charges against Carol at Actors Equity Association, requesting disciplinary action. She had refused to submit the matter to arbitration, and now it had become Equity's hot potato. Carol, in turn, filed countercharges against the producers, asking Equity to "deprive Osterman and Styne of their right to act as producers in the theatre for attempting to destroy me as a performer and for attacking my personal and professional integrity." Equity had no choice but to reject her allegation. Instead it appointed a committee to consider the producers' charges.

The situation was exacerbated further by Carol's continued appearances on "The Entertainers," even though these had been filmed prior to her hospitalization. Adolph Green expressed surprise at seeing her hit in the face with a pie and having a door fall on her head on the TV show. At a press conference in her apartment, Carol, wearing a surgical collar, attempted to refute this accusation by explaining, "The thing with the door was done with a camera angle and a sound effect. And I'd like to say to Adolph that I've never been hit with a pie in my life."

She admitted that she was "unhappy and dissatisfied with the musical long before last July," and acknowledged that she tried to buy her way out "for as high as I could have afforded. Right now I'm mad at all of them. They are harassing me in an attempt to get a money settlement, although the show has closed through no fault of my own. I don't like to fight. You know what? Jule Styne is still my favorite composer, though I should bite my tongue for saying it." She added that she would call a truce if an agreement could be reached "with some degree of reasonableness—but I don't think these people are capable of reasoning."

The Equity committee began to hold a protracted series of hearings. More than ten such sessions were held. While these were going on, Carol, much improved, returned to "The Entertainers" on December 28. I gave up all hope that she would ever come back to *Fade Out—Fade In*.

Then, in early February, almost three months after the suspension of performances, Osterman called to say that Carol, at the urging of Equity, had capitulated. She had agreed to return to the show in a few days. Although it would cost an additional $100,000, he and Styne were determined to reopen. He asked me to coordinate an announcement with Carol's representative, which I cheerfully did. In a matter of hours I issued the following statement from her:

> My doctors, including an orthopedic specialist, will now permit me to return, although they said there is, of course, a risk of recurrence of my neck injury. The doctors said that the choice of returning to the show was mine to make. I have always told Lester Osterman that I would return as soon as the doctors would permit me to. Accordingly, I informed Lester that if he wants to reopen *Fade Out—Fade In*, I will do my utmost to perform in it.

It was not a statement to inspire the confidence of

theatregoers, but it was the best I could do since it was virtually dictated to me by the legal experts.

Frantic preparations were made for a February 15 resumption at the Hellinger. As part of the settlement, the authors agreed to clarify and trim the story about the unknown who accidently becomes a movie star; now she was an usherette instead of a Broadway chorus girl. Carol agreed to take a cut in salary to make possible the engagement of comedian Dick Shawn to replace her former leading man, Jack Cassidy, who had grown tired of waiting and taken another job.

In an attempt to renew interest in this battered property, I composed a brazen ad whose bold-lettered headline read: "CAROL BURNETT IS COMING BACK!" I followed this with what I thought was a persuasive message:

> When *Fade Out—Fade In* was forced to close because of Miss Burnett's illness, it was playing to capacity audiences. Tickets were difficult to obtain. This situation is no longer true. Right now, you have first choice. There are no theatre parties. There is no "million-dollar" advance sale. All tickets are available to the public on a first-come-first-served basis. The opportunity to get GOOD tickets for a HIT musical for current dates is unprecedented.

I did not win an award for copywriting that year.

The *Times* of February 16, 1965, reported: "Peace reigns at *Fade Out—Fade In*, which resumed last night after a 13-week shutdown. After a contractual dispute, the settlement restored employment for 171 persons." Osterman was quoted as saying, "We are trying to avoid acrimony. We want everybody to kiss and make up."

This story does not have a happy ending. Despite my energetic promotional efforts, the box office reaction was disappointing. The events of the previous few months had made the public wary. Theatregoers felt that purchasing tickets was too much of a gamble. On April 17, Osterman and Styne, weary from the fray, and having failed to balance the budget, closed *Fade Out—Fade In* forever after 271 performances, at a loss of $500,000.

A week after the closing, while engaging in informal athletic activity with her husband's children, Carol Burnett tripped and broke an ankle. I cannot say that the news provided much cheer for Osterman and Styne, but I doubt if they ever sent her a "get well" card.

As for me, I wanted to get away—as far from Broadway and the blinding glitter of its stars as I could. I booked a trip to the remotest part of Scandinavia. On my first night at a small Norwegian inn on the fringes of Lapland, a trio was entertaining a handful of guests. As I entered the room, they began to play an off-key medley of Broadway show tunes. It started off, just as you might guess, with "Hey, Look Me Over," from the score of *Wildcat*.

16

Fits and Misfits

The thing that sets me apart from all other theatrical publicists is a never-to-be-broken record that I alone possess. It dismays me that it is not included in the *Guinness Book of World Records*. It is a pity that there is no Hall of Fame in which such achievements can be immortalized.

I have publicized three Broadway plays that took place in candy stores.

It seems fitting that I was selected for these rare assignments. During my growing-up years in the Washington Heights section of Manhattan, when the school year ended and other children were packed off to the sylvan serenity of summer camps, I gravitated to the neighborhood candy store. It was the social center of my early life. It was also where I acquired my persistent taste for the perfect "egg cream"—that supreme, eggless chocolate soda—as well as for Baby Ruths, licorice shoelaces, and Hershey Bars without nuts. (I hate nuts.)

The first of the candy-store plays was called, appropriately enough, *The Garden of Sweets,* by the then-and-still-unknown Buffalo playwright, Waldemar Hansen. It starred the famous Greek actress Katina Paxinou (remember her as Pilar in the film of Hemingway's *For Whom The Bell Tolls?*) as the proprietress of a sweet-shop in Buffalo and mother to a nuisance of a family. The delectable memories of my early life, evoked by *The Garden of Sweets,* were short-lived. It opened and closed at the Anta Theatre on October 31, 1961. Some people said it should have closed during the first intermission. In a statement that I have never heard before or since, Miss Paxinou's husband, the Greek director Alexis Minotis, referred to the play as "defecatingly bad."

I had to wait only three years for my next trip down memory lane. This time it was William Hanley's play, *Slow Dance on the Killing Ground.* The British actor, George Rose, played the German owner of a Brooklyn candy store whose shady past included a job as a locomotive engineer driving trainloads of Jewish prisoners into concentration camps back in the old country. Clarence Williams III played a menacing black whose past was vague. A murky, problematic play, *Slow Dance* aimlessly pirouetted through eighty-eight performances and folded.

Almost eight years to the day passed before Paul Zindel's *The Secret Affairs of Mildred Wild* entered my life. Maureen Stapleton was Zindel's candy-store mistress. This shop was in Greenwich Village, and Miss Stapleton played a foolish sloven of a woman who read all the movie magazines in the store's racks while her husband developed diabetes from eating all the unsold Charlotte Russes. Fortunately for Lee Wallace, who played the husband, the play closed after twenty-three performances, or he would have become a diabetic.

These three failures provided me with about enough income to buy a little penny candy. But what I regret most is my failure to purchase some of the props and set pieces after each had terminated its run. I would have had enough junk to open my own candy store.

When I shave in the morning, I like to listen to the news on the radio. This time a bulletin alarmed me so that I scraped my face from sideburn to ·chin. The report said that Hume Cronyn had been missing for twenty-four hours while on a fishing trip in Bahamian waters. An airsea search had been thus far unsuccessful.

Cronyn is not only a fine actor, but an avid sportsman and expert boatman as well. Only a few weeks earlier, Zander Hollander, a sportswriter for the now-defunct *World-Telegram*, had called seeking a celebrity familiar with boats for an interview on water safety. I suggested Cronyn, a valued client. Hollander agreed and was astounded by Cronyn's thorough knowledge of boatmanship. The actor even prepared a list of safety devices one should have on board before shoving off.

I had hardly wiped the shaving cream from my face when the phone rang. It was Hume's wife, Jessica Tandy. "In case you haven't heard, Hume's been found and he's fine," she said.

"A minute ago I heard he was lost," I said.

"They found him at 6:00 this morning. As soon as he reached shore, he called me and asked me to get hold of you right away."

"I'm grateful to you for calling and relieving my mind," I said.

"Hume and his friends sat in that boat all night," she said. "Planes flew over, and boats went by. But nobody saw them."

"Well, thank God, they were found," I said.

"Hume wants you to call that nice man from the *World-Telegram* who did the interview on safety measures. Tell him that Hume left one thing off the list—a flashlight. If he'd had one on board, he could have signaled for help during the night."

(Telephone conversation with Katharine Hepburn, June 1960)

ME: *Newsweek* would like to interview you about your

forthcoming role of Cleopatra at Stratford.

KH: Absolutely not. It's enough that I'm doing the part this summer. I don't have to do this for a living.

ME: I do, Miss Hepburn.

KH: Very well. I'll do it.

＝＝＞ː＜＝＝

Daniel Blum, in his annual photographic compendium of theatrical activity, *Theatre World,* wrote: "The 1962-63 season was a disastrous one both financially and artistically [ed. note: so what else is new?]. Over six million dollars went down the drain in flops. Among the established playwrights were many failures. Tennessee Williams's *The Milk Train Doesn't Stop Here Anymore* . . . failed at the box office."

Williams's *Milk Train* dealt with an itinerant maker of mobiles who comes to visit a wealthy woman dying of an incurable disease in her sumptuous Italian villa. Hermione Baddeley played the central role in this Roger L. Stevens production, which lingered for sixty-nine performances.

Williams, however, did not accept failure. He continued to polish *Milk Train,* and the following season, it was produced again on Broadway, this time with Tallulah Bankhead as the dying woman, and David Merrick as producer. It ran but five performances.

After the Baltimore tryout premiere, Merrick had said to me, "I can't bring this show in. It still doesn't work. We'll play out our time here and close. I just wanted to produce a Tennessee Williams play."

But he was prevailed upon by Williams, his agent Audrey Wood, and Miss Bankhead to take it all the way to Broadway.

Almost ten years later, Merrick and Stevens joined forces to present Williams's *Out Cry.* In a reminiscent mood, Stevens, now head of the John F. Kennedy Center for the Performing Arts in Washington, recalled his production of *Milk Train.* Playing a game of one-upmanship, he chided

Merrick in front of me by stating, "My production ran longer than yours. I guess I had a better press agent."

I had to remind him that I was the press agent of both productions. "Apart from Williams himself," I said, "I was the only one aboard both sections of the *Milk Train*."

(Conversation in a Washington restaurant, November, 1962)

WAITER: It's been a pleasure serving you, Mr. Perkins.

ANTHONY PERKINS: Thank you. I have no cash or credit cards with me. May I sign the check?

WAITER: Of course, Mr. Perkins. Do you have some kind of identification—like a driver's license?

I have been privileged during my career to work with most of the great photographers: Yousuf Karsh, Richard Avedon, Irving Penn, Milton Greene, Gjon Mili, Philippe Halsman, Martha Swope. But none of them can match Sammy Siegel in one respect—his mismanagement of common everyday speech.

Sammy, who switched from the furniture business to photography, shoots everything—shows, celebrities, inanimate objects, and the English language. I once brought him to the St. James Theatre on a night when Luci Baines and Lynda Byrd Johnson, daughters of the incumbent president, were in the audience watching their friend, Carol Channing, in *Hello, Dolly!* "I'll invite them backstage, Sammy," I said, "and you grab a quick shot."

At the end of the performance, the Johnson girls accepted my invitation. "Did you get the shot of the girls, Sammy?" I asked. "No," he replied, "I couldn't. They were surrounded by Social Security men."

The cultural apex of Sammy's career occurred when I commissioned him to photograph *Henry IV, Part One* at the American Shakespeare Festival. He studied the play and watched two performances, setting up each shot in his mind. At the photo call, Sammy, with supreme confidence, marshalled the actors into position for his pictures. "In the next shot," he ordered, "I want the Oil of North Humberland, his son Henry Poicy, also known as Hutspah, and his daughter-in-law, Mrs. Hutspah."

When he photographed the brother-and-sister twins, Sebastian and Viola, in *Twelfth Night*, Sammy commented, "It's amazing how much these two actors look alike—like two peas in a pot."

Negotiating a deal with Sammy is a war of nerves that he invariably wins. "I'm sticking to my guts," he'll say. "That's my black-bottom price."

Borrowing from Richard Brinsley Sheridan, we began to refer to Sammy's verbal goodies as Samaprops. "Go to the pier, board the ship, and photograph Peter Ustinov," I once instructed him. "Who's gonna give me the proper credidentials?" he asked.

Once, after a late night's shooting, we repaired to a delicatessen for sustenance. After downing a sizable corned beef sandwich and wiping his mouth with a napkin, Sammy commented, "I ate so much I gouged myself."

Not even the national shame of Richard Nixon was exempt from the Samaprop. "He got what he deserved," he said. "He was guilty of a construction of justice. That dope killed the goose from gander."

Sammy, though, takes good pictures, and he's all heart. Discussing an associate whose attributes have never been fully recognized, he said, "Don't worry. He'll get his justly dessert. It'll reach him, either when he dies, or posthumously, whichever comes first."

<hr />

(A production conference in a suite in the Ritz-Carlton Hotel, Boston, September, 1957)

DAVID MERRICK *(to the author of a recently opened musical)*: I'm bringing in Joe Stein to help out with the book.

AUTHOR: Oh, no, you're not.

MERRICK: Oh, yes, I am.

AUTHOR: *(shouting as he leaves the suite)*: I hate you, I hate you, I hate you, I hate all of you. *(Slams door as he exits.)*

MERRICK: Now that he's gone, let's get to work.

(The door opens and author's head reappears.)

AUTHOR: But I want all of you to love me.

The Romans threw Christians to the lions. In the Middle Ages encumbered knights attempted to bend each other's armor and limbs in savage jousts. During the French Revolution cackling hags shrieked in delight as the guillotine neatly separated heads from torsos. The killing of a bull in the ring inevitably brings a Spaniard to his feet in ecstatic admiration, either for the bull's courage—or the matador's luck. Throughout history such sado-masochistic encounters have played to full houses. I have often wondered why tickets aren't sold to the modern equivalent— the talent audition. True, the demand for tickets to *A Chorus Line*, a musical about auditions, is intense, but I'm talking about selling the real thing.

Granted, the comparison is somewhat exaggerated. After all, nobody was ever killed outright at an audition; suicides may have occurred in the aftermaths, however.

I attended several auditions for the very first show with which I was involved, *Finian's Rainbow*. I was curious, green, and totally romantic about every aspect of the theatre in those days. The sight of hundreds of young men and women, however, being rejected without so much as an opportunity to sing one note or dance one step, made me physically ill. "You, you, you, and you may leave," said the director, pointing to innumerable terror-ridden applicants who were either too tall, too short, too fat, too thin, too young, too old, too black, too white. Who knows how much latent star material is extinguished in this manner?

At her early auditions, the teenage Barbra Streisand, out of sheer tension, would talk incessantly from the stage to the shadowy judges seated in the darkened theatre. This tactic, no doubt, was to delay the moment of truth, but it had to be irksome to those who, in a limited period of time, had to appraise hundreds of other aspirants in this show-business slave market. That she was able eventually to make an impression is a tribute to her extraordinary talent. Wild horses could not pry from me the name of the producer who, witnessing Miss Streisand's chattering attempts to establish a rapport with the decision makers, summoned his casting director and muttered angrily, "I told you I don't want ugly girls in my show."

It isn't all fun and games for the "wrecking crew," as actors sometimes refer to the auditioners. Tedium is the norm at most auditions. Listening for an entire day to an assortment of actors reading the same passage from a play can numb the senses. Nor is the endless repetition of "I Could Have Danced All Night," a popular audition song, any more enlivening.

The audition atmosphere is bleak: an empty theatre usually lit by a single harsh overhead worklight illuminating a bare stage and a peeling back brick wall. In the summer the air conditioning is rarely turned on unless the producer has some clout with the theatre owner. In the winter a penetrating chilly dampness can stifle the most incandescent talent.

For all of the aforementioned reasons, I have consistently avoided auditions since those early days. I would accede to a producer's wishes to send out an audition announcement to the proper organs, but it went no further than that. Therefore, it surprised me more than anybody when, pressed for a stunt with which to publicize the 1956 musical, *Li'l Abner,* based on Al Capp's comic strip, I came up with the idea of holding an audition.

The script of *Li'l Abner* called for the character of Moonbeam McSwine to be escorted throughout the performance by a pig. My audition would be for pigs.

Accordingly, I sent out the appropriate release announcing the time and place that two pigs would be selected for Broadway stardom, one for the role of Salomey, the other as understudy. Enchanted with the idea, the newspapers gave my story extensive coverage. I had visions of thousands of pigs appearing at the St. James Theatre on the designated morning. But to hedge my bet I sent an emissary to Secaucus, New Jersey, to alert the pig farmers in the area. And to protect my flanks, I brought in some ringers. These were provided by an enthusiastic young couple, Bernie and Lorraine D'Essen, who ran Animal Talent Scouts, an organization that provided all sorts of trained animals for television, films, opera, and the theatre.

Press attendance was heavy on the morning of the audition. The reporters and cameramen outnumbered the pigs. Only six porkers appeared, two entries from a man who claimed he was the mayor of Secaucus, and four from my friends, Bernie and Lorraine.

Bulbs flashed as the six pigs ran crazily around the St. James, leaving deposits on the stage and in the orchestra. "How do I tell one pig from another?" asked Michael Kidd, the director, whom I had persuaded to make the final choice. "Don't ask me," I replied. "I don't even eat pork."

Kidd wisely selected two of Bernie and Lorraine's entries. He also signed up the D'Essens to provide geese, basset hounds, and a donkey for the show.

As a publicity stunt, my pig audition was a great success. After reading the papers the next morning, Kidd called me and said, "You're lousy with actors, but you're terrific with pigs."

<hr/>

(Telephone conversation between Bob Ullman, a member of my staff, and a Ticket Chiseler from a weekly suburban paper, April, 1964)

ULLMAN: No, you can't have a pair of passes to *Any Wednesday*. It's still selling out. And stop bombarding me

with phone calls. You're a dull bore and a *schnorrer*, and I never want to speak to you again. . . . *(Slams down phone. It rings again and he picks it up.)*
TICKET CHISELER: Bob, we were cut off . . .

My wife and I were leaving on a trip to England. While in London, I planned to see several plays that I might be handling when they were subsequently imported to Broadway. I called my accountant to ask what steps had to be taken to write off the trip. "Get a letter from one of your producers directing you to go to London to do some advance research on a play he's bringing over," he advised.

I telephoned Lewis Allen, a producer who, in the upcoming season, was to present Duerrenmatt's *The Physicists*, which had just been directed by Peter Brook for the Royal Shakespeare Company. "Sure," he said. "Go see Brook in London. As for the letter, just dictate what you want to my secretary, and we'll mail it to you at your London hotel."

Using the most pompously legal-sounding terms at my command, I dictated the letter and, supremely satisfied with myself, packed my bags and left for Britain. After three weeks of restful and mindless driving through the provinces, we checked into our London hotel, the Waldorf, on the Aldwych. A letter from Lewis Allen awaited me. I opened it and after absorbing its officious contents, turned to my wife and said, "Damn that Lew Allen. I'm on my vacation and he's dreamed up some work for me to do. He wants me to see Peter Brook about *The Physicists*."

"Isn't that your own letter?" she asked.

"My God, you're right," I replied, looking upward. "Forgive me, Lew. I'd better go just to make it look good to Internal Revenue."

I went to the stage door of the Aldwych Theatre, London home of the Royal Shakespeare Company, and asked for Brook. " 'E's around the corner rehearsing a new play," said the stage doorman, directing me to an ancient loft building behind the Aldwych. Climbing a rickety flight of stairs, I found myself in a large room. There, behaving like absolute lunatics and wearing the most grotesque makeup I had ever seen, were forty or so actors being marshalled about by Brook. I waited for a break and then went over to Brook to introduce myself. He was distracted, but extremely cordial. Noticing my quizzical expression, he explained that he was rehearsing a play called *The Persecution and Assassination of Jean Paul Marat as Performed by the Inmates of the Asylum at Charenton Under the Direction of the Marquis de Sade*, by the German playwright Peter Weiss. The mere pronouncement of that title took up most of the time we had for our brief, directionless conversation. I left knowing little more about *The Physicists* than when I had entered.

The Physicists failed in New York, but the following season I publicized the play that Brook had been rehearsing in London. To conserve typewriter ribbons, I took the liberty of shortening the title to *Marat/Sade*. It was a big hit on Broadway. And Brook received great acclaim for his innovative staging. He had had his actors spend a few days at an asylum outside London, observing the behavior of the patients there. The performances were frighteningly real.

Oh, yes, Internal Revenue disallowed my 1964 travel expenses to London. They had the nerve to claim that a vacation is not deductible, no matter how many shows and rehearsals I attended.

(Telephone conversation with Lauren Bacall sometime in the run of Cactus Flower, *1966)*

BACALL: How come you never visit me in my dressing room anymore?

ME: *(softly, hand over mouthpiece)* Because you're always nudging me. *(removing hand from mouthpiece, and*

with feigned exuberance) I'll be there tonight, Betty,
before curtain time. I've had a cold and didn't want to
give it to you.

⊱⋅⊰

The First Drama Quartet was never as famous as the
Four Horsemen of Notre Dame, but the individual names
of that distinguished foursome will live longer than the
Fighting Irish's Harry Stuhldreher, Elmer Layden, Jim
Crowley, and Don Miller. They were Charles Laughton,
Charles Boyer, Agnes Moorehead, and Sir Cedric Hard-
wicke, and as The First Drama Quartet, they were pre-
sented by producer Paul Gregory in a reading of Bernard
Shaw's *Don Juan in Hell.* Gregory had organized and per-
fected a cross-country circuit of one-night stands, and The
First Drama Quartet was playing to standing-room-only
houses everywhere.

In 1951, while I was working for Karl Bernstein, he
agreed to publicize the group's only scheduled New York
dates, two evenings at Carnegie Hall. A one-nighter is a
labor of love for a press agent; a two-nighter is two labors
of love. The publicist has to work just as hard as if he were
handling a standard engagement, while receiving very little money for his effort.

Since the closest this attraction would come to New
York before the Carnegie Hall dates was a single performance in, of all places, White Plains, New York, Karl decided that he and I should catch the show there. Gregory
suggested that we arrive early, have dinner with the stars,
then see them in action on the stage of the RKO Keith's, a
barn of a movie house converted to legit for the one night
only.

We arrived on schedule, and after the usual introductions, the six of us headed for the only presentable restaurant near the theatre, Schrafft's. As we entered, the gray-
haired hostess gasped in excitement at the sight of these
four prominent stars. "This is the greatest thing that ever
happened to Schrafft's White Plains," she said.

Boyer corrected her. "The greatest thing that could ever happen to Schrafft's White Plains would be larger portions," he said in his famous French accent.

The pre-theatre conversation was stilted. The actors obviously had their minds on that night's performance, but we were able to set the publicity ground rules for New York. Later, backstage, the stage manager warned us, "Watch out for Boyer. He's a hypochondriac. Before every performance he puts a thermometer in his mouth and another up his behind. If they don't read the same, he won't go on."

We watched the beautifully controlled performance; four artists working together with perfection. Sir Cedric had the fewest lines. Afterwards I asked him how he kept his concentration. He replied, "I count the freckles on Agnes's back."

The British actor-playwright-director Peter Ustinov made his American stage debut in 1957 in his own play, *Romanoff and Juliet.* I was aware that Ustinov was a man of great wit and intelligence, but his reputation had not yet reached the American theatregoing public. Publicity exposure in advance of the opening was essential. Misguidedly, perhaps, I thought a touch of color should be dabbed on the Ustinov personality; even a touch of eccentricity. After a brainstorming session in my office, it was decided to make Ustinov a lover of rare animals. Put an animal or a child in a photograph and it's a sure break in the papers. But what kind of animal should we use?

I decided to seek inspiration at the Central Park Zoo, which used to be a pleasant place to spend a few hours, particularly during a working day. There I spotted a pair of koala bears. I detest the word "cute," but koala bears are cute. If only I could get two koala bears, I thought. We'd name one Romanoff and the other Juliet.

I rushed back to the office and called my experts in these matters, Lorraine and Bernie D'Essen. "Forget about koala bears," they advised. "You've just seen two of the only six in New York. The other four are in the Bronx Zoo. But we *can* help you out with two wombats. We just got them from a friend in Australia who told us that there aren't any others in the entire United States. Wombats are first cousins to koalas; they're even cuter."

"You've got a deal. I want those wombats," I said, and I outlined my plan to them.

In the best spy fashion, my cover story began to take shape: Ustinov arrives from England by ship; he sends his pet wombats ahead by plane; a friend brings them to the pier to meet him; he is eager to see them again because he loves them so. The perfect plan!

Since Ustinov was already en route aboard the Queen Elizabeth, I wired him an outline of our harmless caper, advising that I would be bringing two wombats to the ship. Within a few hours I received a reply that said merely, "Bring two of everything." It was signed "Noah."

Wombats, Lorraine, photographers, reporters, and Queen Elizabeth converged at the Hudson River pier at the prescribed time. By prearrangement, we were permitted to board and met Ustinov on an upper deck. I made the usual introductions, and then Lorraine, posing as Peter's great and good friend, thrust the two cuddly bundles into the bearded actor's arms. "What the devil are these?" he sputtered.

No more uncomfortable threesome was ever photographed—a tangle of furry animals and furry actor struggling to be free of each other. After everybody had left, Ustinov turned to me and said, "Got your wire and thought you were jesting, old boy. I detest animals."

(Telephone conversation with a producer, winter, 1973)
PRODUCER: I have your Boston expense account in front of me, and I see you're charging me a dollar for flight insurance. Tell me, who was the beneficiary?
ME: My wife.

PRODUCER: I refuse to pay the dollar unless I'm the beneficiary.

I crossed paths with Walter Matthau several times during his Broadway stage career, which for a long time had more downs than ups. He was in two of the biggest turkeys I ever publicized, but surely Matthau was blameless. He never gave a bad performance that I can remember, but those plays were hopeless.

On one occasion he visited me in my office to suggest that I do his personal publicity. I realized that there was no way he could pay me. He wasn't working at the time, and I had also heard that his gambling debts were astronomical. A poor risk, as the insurance actuaries would say. Trying to let him down gently, I said, "Walter, your timing is off. Let's wait until you get a smash hit. Then we can get together and work out a deal."

We left it at that and did not see each other until four years later when we were both involved with Neil Simon's *The Odd Couple*, a blockbuster. Walter gave a sensational performance as Oscar Madison, a sloppy sportswriter, in a perfectly paired duet with Art Carney as the prissy Felix Unger, a nut on tidiness. Simon must have had Matthau in mind for the part from the day he started to write the play.

Walter won the Tony Award that season. It was the triumph of his career. Once known as a "jinx" actor, he was now the hottest figure on Broadway. Because it is unethical for the press agent of a show to be, at the same time, the paid personal publicist of any one actor in the cast, I could not say to Walter that the time had come for us to make some arrangement. In my capacity as the show's publicist, however, I was obligated to publicize him to the hilt anyway. It was not a difficult job; he had been largely ignored in the past by the media and was now the most sought-after interview subject.

When his contract with *The Odd Couple* was completed, Matthau went to Hollywood as a full-fledged star with a fat contract. He won the Academy Award as Jack Lemmon's conniving brother-in-law in Billy Wilder's *The Fortune Cookie*. It was then that I decided to drop him a short note. "The time is now," I wrote. "I'm ready to become your personal press agent."

His brief reply read: "Screw you. I'll see you on the way down."

(Telephone conversation between Matthau and his agent, Lee Stevens, of the William Morris Agency)

MATTHAU: I just bought a new Rolls Royce. Here in California I can get a special license plate for a small extra fee, but it's limited to six characters. You got any suggestions?

STEVENS: R-E-N-T-E-D.

Stringent rules have all but eliminated the practice, but for many years personalities making appearances on radio and television talk shows could realize a little extra income by working in the names of certain products. There existed a group of operators who made a living by arranging for celebrities to mention commercial items. Standard rates of payment prevailed for local radio and TV shows, and for network mentions. A few deftly dropped names could bring up to $300.

Walter Slezak, then starring in *Fanny*, was delighted when he heard of this apparently accepted form of payola. It was far short of grand larceny. He was always in great demand on the talk shows because of his sense of humor and superior intellect. None of these programs, however, paid a fee. Slezak reasoned that there was nothing wrong if, while plugging the play in which he was appearing, he plugged something else, too. It would recompense him for the effort it took to come into the city from his home in Larchmont to appear at a broadcast studio.

Within a short time Walter became notorious for his product mentions. It was a simple matter for him to give the name of a reducing-and-diet firm known as Slenderella by referring to his own girth and to his desperate need to trim off the excess poundage at a certain reducing parlor. Since he could slip in plugs with lightning speed, interviewers became increasingly nervous when Slezak appeared on their shows. Too many mentions could jeopardize them with their own sponsors.

Mike Wallace had just started a new television show in which he put his guests through a great deal of embarrassment with loaded questions about closet skeletons. An ex-actor, he was beginning to develop the style that later was to make him a top newscaster. Despite the sometimes excruciating pain of Wallace's grilling, most personalities were too egocentric to refuse an invitation. Slezak had been invited to appear, but was advised by my partner, Lee Solters, to turn down the request.

"He'll nail you on all those plugs," Lee told him.

"Don't worry," assured Slezak. "I can handle *him*. If it gets out of hand, I'll change the subject."

The interview started off pleasantly enough. For a while the questions were benign and mainly biographical. Then Wallace abruptly switched to the subject of payola. Slezak immediately interrupted, "Let's talk about my interest in astrology and drop that boring stuff. Last night my wife and I did your horoscope, Mike. It was most revealing. We learned that your marriage to that lovely Buffy Cobb was on the rocks. It also told us that after much floundering, your career might be on the right track, because you'll never make it as an actor. Stick with television."

With a few words Slezak had switched the course of the interview. Wallace never thought to return to the subject of plugs and on-the-side money again. When it was all over, he said, "Walter, you were very clever."

Slezak smiled and said, "Mike, it was an over-the-weight match."

Edward R. Murrow eagerly accepted Slezak as a guest on his prestigious TV show, "Person-to-Person," whose format involved live coverage of notables in their own homes. As the cameras followed the celebrity from room to room, Murrow fired questions from the studio. It was all very friendly and comfortable.

On the day of the telecast, Lee received a call from Murrow's producer. "Tell your man that this is a class show. No mentions *whatsoever,* of *any* product! He's become the talk of the industry, and we don't want him screwing around on *our* show."

Slezak was advised of the call, and he vowed that he would play it straight. That night Murrow's cameras picked up Walter in his basement playroom. He and Murrow discussed everything from art to acting. Walter was never more personable. He revealed himself as the *gemütlich* man of culture and breeding. At a prearranged point Slezak said to Murrow, "Let's go upstairs now, Ed, and meet my lovely family."

The cameras followed him up a narrow staircase, through a hallway, and into an attractively decorated living room. There, seated at a bridge table, was Walter's wife Kaasi, his son, and his two daughters. 'Just look at them, Ed. My lovely wife and lovely children—and they're playing JOTTO!"

$$\rightleftharpoons\!\!\vdots\!\!\rightleftharpoons$$

(Telephone conversation with David Merrick, spring, 1972)

ME: David, the Associated Press is doing a piece on the Women's Lib movement, and they want your thinking on the subject.

MERRICK (after a short pause): Woman's place is *in* the oven.

$$\rightleftharpoons\!\!\vdots\!\!\rightleftharpoons$$

I cannot truly say that I knew Billy Rose. But the Bantum Barnum, as he was called in the columns, once gained temporary custody over me.

In 1964 Merrick presented the musical, *Foxy,* by Ian McLellan Hunter, Ring Lardner, Jr., Johnny Mercer, and Robert Emmett Dolan. Suggested by Ben Jonson's *Volpone,* it starred Bert Lahr and Larry Blyden. Jonson's tale of greed and chicanery was set in Venice; *Foxy* took place in the Klondike.

Merrick opened the show in Cleveland where, on viewing the first preview, he decided the best course of action would be to disown it. He offered to give it, free of charge, to his general manager Jack Schlissel and me. Whether or not it was a legitimate offer, I cannot tell, but my mother taught me never to accept gifts from strangers or disgruntled producers.

Although Lahr was supremely funny, and Blyden the prefect foil for him, the show wasn't much. After limping through tryouts in Cleveland and Detroit, it opened at Billy Rose's Ziegfeld Theatre in New York.

When the curtain fell on opening night, Merrick fled to the Oak Room of The Plaza for a late supper. There he ran into his landlord and Howard Reinheimer, the theatrical attorney. "I liked your show a lot, David," said Billy. "Want to sell me a piece?"

Aware that the notices were lukewarm, Merrick so advised Rose, who nevertheless was still interested. "You can take over the whole thing for $10,000," Merrick said.

Rose accepted the deal on the spot and had Reinheimer draw up and witness a rough contract. He also wrote out a check to Merrick. From that point on, I was working for Billy Rose, who inherited all existing *Foxy* contracts.

Merrick exhorted me to toil hard in Rose's service. "He's a great promoter," he said. "Maybe he can pull it off and get a decent run out of the show."

The next morning Rose summoned me to his palatial East Side townhouse. I responded eagerly. Not only was I breathlessly awaiting his words of wisdom on theatrical salesmanship, but I'd also been told that his art and sculpture collection was something to see.

The art lived up to expectations, but the fires of promotional genius for which Rose had become famous were banked now. I found him sitting alone in his oversized living room nervously clutching a tape that emerged from a working stock-market ticker. Rose was also an investment wizard. "What ideas do you have for the show?" he asked, without looking up from the tape.

Although in my heart I knew that *Foxy* was a terminal case, I outlined an aggressive and expensive promotional campaign that included a series of breezy columns to be written by him. It was a successful device that he had used with past productions and nightclubs he owned.

Perhaps it was the result of something he read on those tapes, but he looked me in the eye and barked, "I don't want to spend a lot of money. And I'm not up to writing those columns. See what you can get for nothing and we'll talk in a few days."

My audience with Billy Rose was over, and I left knowing little more than when I came. He even failed to give me a single stock tip.

Within a week Billy began to share my vision of ultimate disaster. *Foxy* was dying at the box office and he would have liked his $10,000 back from Merrick. But it was too late. Merrick announced that he was donating the money to Rose's favorite charity, the America-Israel Cultural Foundation, earmarking it for the National Museum of Israel. Billy's five-figured gamble had become Merrick's tax deduction.

<hr/>

(*Conversation in the Stage Delicatessen between British star Albert Finney, a waiter, and me, September, 1963*)

FINNEY: Bring me a salt beef and chips, please.

WAITER: Don't you know how to talk the King's English, buddy?

ME: He means he wants a corned beef sandwich with French fries.

WAITER: So why didn't he say so?

17

Executive Privilege

Quadrennially, I clean out my desk drawers. I mean to do it every year, but I am not one of those admirable people who insert everything in orderly manila folders, preserving them for posterity in steel filing cabinets. As an archivist I am a failure. My desk drawers are my filing cabinets.

Four years are about right. By then it is well-nigh impossible to open the drawers without a great deal of effort. The piles of cancelled checks, paid bills, letters, copies of tax returns, dried-up ballpoint pens, travel brochures, and used typewriter ribbons have reached the top. I would much prefer to buy a new desk, but common sense dictates that the time is at hand to sort things out, to throw away those items that will not affect my future well-being.

Recently I devoted an entire Sunday to this onerous task. I had filled several trash pails to the brim when I came across a letter from the White House that prompted me to summon my wife. "Did I ever show you this?" I asked, handing her the neatly typed document.

The letter read:

March 4, 1970

Dear Mr. Sabinson:

The February 22 performance of *1776* made the evening one of the most memorable in White House history, and I want to express my thanks to you and to your assistants for the time and effort you devoted to the arrangements for this presentation. I particularly appreciate your kindness in making the *1776* records and programs available for our guests.

Mrs. Nixon and I were pleased to have the opportunity to welcome you and Mrs. Sabinson to the White House and we join in sending our best wishes to you.

Sincerely,

Richard Nixon

After absorbing the contents, my wife asked, "What are you going to do with it?"

"Throw it away, of course," I replied.

"Why? It might have some value."

"You're kidding," I said. "There must be thousands of letters signed by Nixon. Who in his right mind would pay good money for it? Isn't it enough that every phone call I made to the White House at that time is probably on tape? Comes the revolution, and somebody finds this letter, we'll have our heads shaved as collaborators. And that would be downright ironic because I've hated the man since he first became a public figure."

"A lot he cares that you hate him," my wife said. "You and 200 million others. Don't throw it away. It hasn't burned a hole in your desk."

Thus convinced, I inserted the letter back in the drawer to become the first item in a new four-year pile.

My brief encounter with Nixon and his minions began in the late winter of 1970 when I was handling the musical, *1776*, by Sherman Edwards and Peter Stone. Stuart Ostrow, the producer, called to advise me that the White House had requested a command performance of his show about the signing of the Declaration of Independence. It was to be given in the presidential mansion on the 238th anniversary of George Washington's birth.

"Turn it down, Stu," I said. "We don't need Nixon. The show's a big hit. We're liable to alienate our audience."

"Why?" he insisted on knowing.

"Because once the mark of Nixon is upon us," I said, "we'll be considered another piece of propaganda. That's not the way I've been selling your show. He needs us to provide some entertainment on what otherwise would be a dull evening in the White House. Anyway, how can you trust a man who wears a little American flag in his lapel?"

"I can't argue with you," Stuart said. "My feelings about Nixon are as strong as yours. But you're letting your politics blur one aspect of this situation. Official recognition of the Broadway theatre has some importance. And what about the publicity? It should be enormous."

"Publicity, shmublicity," I countered, summoning up the best intellectual argument I could manage at the moment. "Turn them down, please, Stu."

"I'm inclined to," he said. "They want an abbreviated version of the show. I've told them nothing doing. Either the whole thing or nothing. If they accept, it'll be the first time a full-length, full-scale Broadway musical has ever been presented in the White House. Don't you grasp the historical significance of the occasion?"

"I hope they refuse," I said. "I've already been to the White House—three times as a tourist, and once when Merrick put on excerpts from *Hello, Dolly!* with Carol Channing for the amusement of LBJ and his friends. I wasn't too crazy about Johnson, but Nixon—c'mon, Stu."

"Don't worry," he said. "Nothing's final yet. I'll call you when I hear from them."

For the next week or so, I prayed daily that Ostrow's proposal would prove unacceptable. No such luck. The White House acceded to his wishes and indicated its pleasure in having the full show from beginning to end. I had no monkey wrench in my kit with which to sabotage the arrangement, and other than quitting, had no choice but to do what Ostrow was paying me to do—render as much publicity from the event as possible.

It was at this point that I decided to psych myself. I would create a fantasy world to fit easily into the ugly reality of the situation. I was scheduled to make several preliminary visits with our manager, Ira Bernstein, to the White House to discuss the logistics of both the performance and the publicity with members of the Nixon staff. But I would not go as Harvey Sabinson, downtrodden, sell-out, sniveling Broadway press agent. I would imagine myself a diplomatic envoy for some small, emerging nation. My mission? To negotiate a favorable image among the world powers for my country, without compromise, and totally free of the strangulating yoke of Nixon America.

At breakfast before my first trip to Washington, I peered over the second section of the *New York Times* and in my best clipped and emotionless James Mason accent, said to my wife, "Don't wait dinner for me, dear. I won't be home until quite late."

"Where are you going today?" she inquired.

"To Washington on the nine o'clock shuttle," I replied, leaking just enough information to whet her interest.

"What for?"

"It's top secret," I said, and resumed reading the paper.

"Oh, come off it and stop playing games."

"It's delicate, dear. My lips are sealed."

"Just as the front door will be when you get back if you don't tell me what it's all about."

"Why can't there be a little dignity around here for a man who in a few hours will be entering the White House to negotiate and resolve a matter of utmost sensitivity?"

"One more pompous statement like that and you're going to get two medium-soft-boiled eggs all over your imaginary striped pants. Now tell me why you're going to Washington."

My resistance had been shattered by this diabolical interrogator, and I spilled the entire story of the impending White House performance of *1776*, confessing my guilt at having to collaborate with the enemy, and begging her forgiveness.

"Don't feel bad, sweetie," she said. "You didn't vote for the man. Besides, you have to look at it this way: you're not doing it for Nixon. You're doing it for your country."

"You mean that?" I said, my spirits brightening perceptibly.

"Of course I do. It should be a great evening. And don't come back unless you get an invitation for me."

I picked up my attaché case, locked an imaginary chain bracelet around my wrist, and headed for LaGuardia Airport in a positive frame of mind. No longer would I envision myself the Judas of Forty-fifth Street.

I determined to retain some elements of my diplomatic identity. Sitting on the plane, I kept saying to myself, "Be reserved. Be cool. Be emotionless. Be precise. Be firm. But most of all, remember to get that invitation for your wife."

The guards at the East Gate of the White House regarded me without suspicion. After I identified myself and they consulted a list, they directed me to the proper entrance. Obviously they had been briefed on the importance of my mission. They didn't even insist on examining the contents of my attaché case, which bore ten pages of background material on *1776*, five copies of the theatre program, and three triangles of Gruyère cheese in the event I was afflicted with hunger pangs at an inopportune moment.

My appointment was with Connie Stuart, press secretary to Mrs. Nixon. A tight-lipped, reserved young woman, she welcomed me to her office with an offer of a cup of coffee. "Is Ron Ziegler joining us?" I asked.

"Oh, no," she replied. "Social functions such as this are my responsibility."

It was plain that the matter was not of top priority. I was getting the second team . . . the third team? For a moment I regretted not sending the kid from my mail room in my place.

Mrs. Stuart advised me that the performance would be given in the historic East Room, for which a stage had been constructed some years back. It would be followed by a champagne reception in the State Dining Room. No working press would be admitted to the actual performance, and only a few journalistic stars would be included in the limited list of 200 guests. My inclination was to scream in pain. How the hell was I going to get maximum national coverage if no working press was there? But then the suave diplomat in me took over. I pointed out that the cast would require a complete dress rehearsal in the afternoon, to which the media could certainly be invited. Mrs. Stuart concurred. I bet she wished she had thought of it first.

I was asked to prepare a complete list of all the performers and production personnel who would be coming to the White House. This was for security clearance. Security clearance? Did court jesters have to be loyal, too? Standard operating procedure, Mrs. Stuart explained.

After a brief discussion of other details and a cursory inspection of the East Room and the dressing room areas below, I departed the White House to exuberant waves of farewell from the guards at the East Gate.

On the plane back to New York it occurred to me that I had neglected to mention that my wife would be accompanying me.

When I reached home that night, my own first lady greeted me by asking, "Well, what kind of day did you have at the White House, Excellency?"

"Highly productive," I replied. "I'm getting everything I want. Millions of dollars in aid and all the publicity I can eat. Nixon was so thrilled that he kissed me on both cheeks and offered me custody of Bebe Rebozo. And Pat, that dear woman, wants to know what you're wearing the night of the White House performance. She told me that she shops at Loehmann's too."

"Did you actually meet the president?"

"He tried to make it, but he was tied up working on the bombing of Cambodia."

"It just shows you that those people don't really know what they're doing if they let a closet subversive like you into the White House," she said. "Did you meet *any* famous people?"

"Oh, sure. A couple of nice security guards, Pat's press secretary, a few stenographers and typists. Nixon doesn't see anybody. He sits alone in the Oval Room thinking of ways to annoy me."

"It doesn't sound very exciting."

"It wasn't."

A few days later we hit a clinker. Some smartass from the White House took the trouble to come up to New York to see *1776*. A call to Ostrow followed, requesting the deletion from the command performance of a song called "Momma, Look Sharp." The song is a ballad sung by a dying soldier; it might be interpreted vaguely, as anti-war. It would offend an overwhelmingly hawkish audience, someone had determined.

But Ostrow held his ground. All or nothing, he insisted. His intransigence was impressive, and the White House backed off. The arrangements were concluded without further disruption.

It dismayed me to learn that I had passed the security clearance. Surely, I thought, my socialist heritage would bar me. What about all those political meetings I had attended in college? All those leaflets passed out? What about the active support I had given to that left-wing menace, Eugene McCarthy, in his wishy-washy drive for the Democratic nomination? What about all the revolutionary thoughts that had swirled about in my brain all my life? They counted for nothing. I was acceptable to the Nixon

White House. The only thing that turned up was the fact that I was married, for the engraved invitation that reached my house was addressed to Mr. and Mrs.

"I'm glad you remembered to take care of it with all that's on your mind," said my wife.

We arrived at the East Gate of the White House at noon of the historic day. The guards greeted me as an old friend. "You know the way, sir," one of them said. My wife was impressed.

The cast had arrived by chartered plane and was gorging itself on a luncheon of meat loaf in the State Dining Room. No matter how any of them felt about Richard Nixon, a sense of excitement ran through the company.

Mrs. Stuart thought it advisable that prior to the dress rehearsal, I speak to the White House press corps to explain what we were doing and to answer any questions. The turnout was, as I expected, enormous. The East Room was virtually filled, television crews all over the place, reporters poised with steno pads at the ready, prepared to record my words for posterity. In a quavering voice, I delivered some gibberish, returned to my seat, and whispered to my wife, "How'd I do?"

"It was momentous," she said. "The first time the press has gotten a straight story in this building since Nixon became president."

During the rehearsal I just sat there, the picture of contentment, confident that every network would carry the piece on both the 6:00 and 11:00 newscasts. With a little bit of luck it would even make the front page of tomorrow's *Times*. (It did, in what was probably the only favorable story Nixon ever received in that publication. He knew what he was doing when he latched on to *1776*.)

When the rehearsal was over, we rushed back to the hotel to watch the news and to don the uniform of the evening. Black tie, the invitation read. I was fumbling, as usual, with my studs, when my wife said to me, "Did you get a chance to look at the guest list?"

"No," I replied. "What about it?"

"I swiped a copy from one of Mrs. Stuart's assistants. Wait till you see the names. Some of your all-time favorites."

"Like who?" I asked.

"Oh, Agnew, Stans, a few dozen heads of what we laughingly call the military-industrial complex."

"Let me see that," I said, grabbing it from her hands.

I glanced through five mimeographed pages of names and affiliations. Chairmen of Republic Steel, Mobil, Gulf, Chase Manhattan, presidential aides, a smattering of governors, cabinet members, generals, lobbyists. All true lovers of the musical theatre. And they had come from such far-off places as Palm Beach, Palm Springs, Dallas, and Greenville, Mississippi. Here and there were a few I'd invite to my own house, such as Senator Mansfield, *Washington Post* drama critic Dick Coe (who I later discovered had suggested *1776* to the White House in the first place), CBS newsman Dan Rather (later to become one of Nixon's *bêtes noires*), and Vince Lombardi, coach of the Washington Redskins. Vince was probably there to pick up next week's game plan from Nixon.

"This is our big chance," I yelled. "When are we going to have another opportunity to tell off some of these people?"

"Make a fool of yourself if you want, but it'll embarrass the actors," she admonished me. "Leave the remarks to people like Eartha Kitt."

When we reached the East Gate, I waved my invitation to the guard who yelled, "Back again? When are you moving in?"

The guests were immediately ushered into the East Room to be seated before the arrival of the Nixons. With the exception of the first row, reserved for the presidential party, we were free to sit anywhere.

"How about here near the door?" I asked my wife.

"It's drafty."

"We'll get a better view of the guests."

We seated ourselves near the door.

Most of the people were unfamiliar to us with the exception of Agnew ("he's taller than I thought") and Stans ("he's shorter than I thought"). Vince Lombardi and his wife sat down next to us. I turned to him and asked, "Is it true that winning is the only thing, Coach?"

"It's better than losing, my friend," he replied, blinding me with his prominent white teeth, which he bared in a broad grin.

Then the Nixons entered, smiling and waving, he ever the candidate, she the self-possessed helpmate. The crowd stood up to applaud. I remained seated until my wife grabbed my arm firmly and forced me upward. "You're hurting me," I said.

"Don't be conspicuous," she said.

I stood, but I did not applaud. Score one for the doves.

After the United States Marine Band played "The Star-Spangled Banner," the performance began. The cast was in top form. Not a line was fluffed, not an entrance missed in these strange surroundings. Two hours, without intermission, passed swiftly. No one in the audience had even coughed or fainted during the rendition of "Momma, Look Sharp."

1776 ends on a high note. The sound of the Liberty Bell is heard as each of the delegates, when his state is called, affixes his signature to that remarkable document hammered out after so many months of anguish and argument. When the last name was written, the audience leaped to its feet and gave the company an ovation.

At this point Nixon walked up on the stage to express his appreciation to the cast, and to Ostrow, Edwards, Stone, and director Peter Hunt. Armed with some historical sidelights, he pointed out that Abigail Adams, the first first lady to inhabit the executive mansion, used to hang her wash in the very room in which we were now standing. "Do you believe that story?" I asked my wife.

Nixon treated us to other goodies. He informed us that John Adams had written a blessing that was carved into the mantelpiece of the State Dining Room, expressing the hope that only wise and just men would live in the White

House. Odd that the man who was telling us this would ultimately render the blessing "inoperative."

The President concluded his "inspirational" address by telling the audience, "The house is yours."

I do not know what exactly he meant by that remark, but the guests immediately lined up to receive handshakes from him and Mrs. Nixon. We were pulled into line by Mrs. Mansfield, who assumed responsibility for our education in White House protocol. "You've never been to one of these things before. I can tell," she said. "They do things differently here. The men go before the women. When you reach the President's military aide, give him your name. He'll whisper it to the President, who'll greet you, and maybe engage in a little small talk. If you answer him, make it brief. He's got to shake a lot of hands."

The line moved quickly. When I reached Nixon, he said, "You're the man who helped with bringing this wonderful show here. I want it back for a performance in the bicentennial year."

I couldn't manage a reply. The thought that he might still be president in 1976 dismayed me. Later it occurred to me that I should have said, "If we're both still running."

Once past the receiving line, we found ourselves in the State Dining Room being served champagne and indeterminate *hors d'oeuvres*. Being strangers at a standup party of board chairmen and assorted sons and daughters of the American Revolution wasn't much fun.

A man who identified himself as Governor Holton of Virginia attempted to elicit from me a commitment to bring the show to the State House in Richmond. I took his phone number, but proceeded to lose it.

The ball was over at midnight for the Broadway Cinderellas. The stage managers herded us into chartered buses to be whisked off to Dulles Airport to the chartered plane that would return us to New York and the real world. Only Howard da Silva remained behind to get a decent night's rest at the Hay-Adams Hotel opposite the White House.

The following morning da Silva looked out his window

to see a group of anti-Vietnam war pickets parading in front of the executive mansion. The man who the night before had portrayed Benjamin Franklin for Nixon and his friends later told me that he hurriedly dressed and joined the picket line.

I was wrong about the White House performance having a negative effect on the run of *1776*. The theatregoing public never held it against us, and the show lived to a ripe old age, as these things go. It didn't last until 1976, but then again neither did the Nixon presidency.

Index